CLASSIC MURDERS OF THE NORTH WEST

Sara Lee

TRUE
CRIME
Library

True Crime Library
A Forum Press Book
by the Paperback Division of
Forum Design,
PO Box 158, London SE20 7QA

An Imprint of True Crime Library
© 1999 Forum Design
© 1999 Sara Lee
All rights reserved

Typeset by Techniset,
86 Market Street, Newton-le-Willows,
Merseyside, WA12 9BW
Printed and bound in Great Britain by
Cox & Wyman Ltd, Reading, Berkshire

ISBN 1 874358 32 X

To my Mum, Winnie,
who has always
been there for me

Other titles in the
TRUE CRIME LIBRARY

CONTENTS

PREFACE

Sara Lee is a crime writer and researcher who was born and brought up in Manchester and has written widely about the history of crime in the area. The increasing popularity of her true crime stories and the success of her first book *Strange Tales From Strangeways* meant that another collection just had to be published.

Classic Murders Of The North West is a selection of gritty murder cases meticulously written which vividly describe the people and landscape of the north west of England.

The book details cases as diverse as *The Congleton Cannibal*, a butcher whose motive for murder was that he had heard that human flesh tasted like pork and wanted to try some, to *Manchester's Canal Boat Murder* and the mysterious last days of Betty Eckersley who had the misfortune of being the girl friend of Tom Done, the handsome bargee.

Sara Lee's descriptions of some of the trials lead the reader down mysterious legal avenues, as in the case of Margaret Messenger, the 14-year-old girl who was sentenced to hang, and *The Coolest Killer* who went to the gallows on circumstantial evidence and the testimony of children, protesting his innocence to the end.

Passions run high in many of the stories but none more so than in the case of 60-year-old Walter Chipperfield, who lost his head over a woman half his age and tragically gunned her down in a Cheshire street.

Unrequited love is often a motive for murder and *Classic*

Murders Of The North West gives full rein to the seething undercurrent of love, lust and need lurking beneath a veneer of social respectability.

Not all the crimes were committed by men — *The Warrington Poisonings* describes a woman who might now be suffering from Munchausen's Syndrome; a young mother who loses two children and then her own mother to the same inexplicable end as she lovingly tends them during their illnesses...

There are mad women, as in the story of Albert Dewhurst, the butcher who would have lived if he hadn't missed his tram, and there are greedy ones — Mrs. Merrifield, *The Blackpool Poisoner* was a snobbish, insensitive housekeeper, who may have got away with murder if she hadn't bragged so much...

The author has cleverly weaved the character and flavour of the north west of England into each case in this classic collection.

1
MANCHESTER'S CANAL-BOAT MURDER

Sweeping her up in his powerful arms, he carried her kicking and screaming onto the barge

HE WAS young and successful. He had everything going for him, but for one weakness. Tom Done, a handsome bargee known to just about everyone on the canals around Manchester, had a way with him that made an impression. He certainly impressed his employers: they had made him a barge captain by the time he was 20. But although he was master of the *Six Brothers*, he couldn't master his hot-tempered jealousy, as one girl in particular had discovered.

Most of his trips were spent carrying cargo along the waterways between Manchester and the Cheshire town of Runcorn, his crew consisting of a newly acquired first mate, Robert Holroyd, a 28-year-old Yorkshireman who attended to most of the chores — stabling the tow-horse, loading and unloading, and on the evening of Sunday, August 27th, 1809, ensuring the barge was safely moored at Manchester's Dale Street wharf.

That accomplished, Holroyd made his way to the Bull's Head. Tom Done arrived later, his paperwork completed, to find his first mate drinking with two fellow-boatmen — William Brookes and a bargee known as "Old David."

The skipper's arrival did not go unnoticed. Sitting nearby was Betty Eckersley with two of her friends —

Sarah Rigby, with whom she shared lodgings, and Martha Hancock. Betty had already downed several glasses of ale. She was feeling jolly, and seeing Done made her even jollier. They had known each other for three years, and although their relationship had cooled due to Done's possessiveness, Betty still had a soft spot for the young captain.

Crossing the room, she perched playfully on his knee and slipped her arm round his neck. Done's response was to order more beer, calling Betty's friends over to join them. Canal boatmen were hard-drinkers who enjoyed a good time between trips, and Tom Done was no exception. Within the next hour he and his friends consumed several gallons of beer, which Done paid for.

Then the party broke up, the men having to make an early start the next morning. As they left the pub Tom slipped his arm round Betty and asked her to return with him to his boat for the night, as she had often done in the past.

Jolly though she was, however, Betty was sober enough to remember the bad times with Tom Done, the occasions when he'd threatened her with violence, accusing her of cheating on him while he'd been away. Now she feared being alone with him, especially after he'd been drinking heavily and old wounds might be reopened.

But Done was persistent. Betty finally agreed to go as far as the boat with him, but only if her friend Sarah came with them. Done seemed happy enough with that and he, Betty, Sarah and Holroyd set off together down Dale Street towards the Rochdale Canal and the *Six Brothers*.

On reaching the wharf Holroyd went straight aboard the boat and below to his bunk, while his three companions lingered on the quayside as Done continued to pressure Betty to join him for the night.

Drunk though she was, she stubbornly refused. But Done was used to being obeyed. Sweeping her up in his powerful arms, he carried her kicking and screaming onto the barge. Sarah, herself more than tipsy, could only look on helplessly through bleary eyes as her friend disappeared still struggling into the dark living-quarters of the boat.

It was a week later when Betty's mother decided to do something about her nagging feeling that something was wrong. She couldn't get Betty out of her mind. Though they were not particularly close and hadn't seen much of each other since Betty left home in January, Mrs. Eckersley felt an urgent need to see her daughter to make sure she was all right. The snag was that she didn't know where she was living.

She decided to seek out her other daughter, Mrs. Tess Walker, and ask her for Betty's address. She found her at a neighbour's, and as luck would have it, she was with Sarah Rigby.

Sarah described the events of the previous Sunday evening which had ended with Tom Done carrying the struggling Betty aboard his boat. She'd seen nothing of Betty since that night, she told Mrs. Eckersley. When her friend didn't come home the following morning she had assumed that on calming down Betty had forgiven Tom for carrying her off and had agreed to accompany him on his trip — something she had done in the past.

Far from being reassured, Mrs. Eckersley was now even more alarmed, knowing what she did of Betty's stormy relationship with Done.

She went at once to convey her fears to the local constable, who promptly launched an inquiry into Betty Eckersley's disappearance. Within hours she knew the worst.

On September 4th Jim Bowden was walking along the canal towpath at the picturesque Cheshire village of Lymm, some 20 miles from Manchester, when he noticed something floating on the water near Lymm Bridge. At first it looked like a dead animal — a common enough sight. Then he realised it was a piece of sacking. Pulling it to the canal bank he was horrified to see the head and shoulders of a woman protruding from it. He quickly man-handled it onto the towpath where he found that the corpse had been weighted with a large stone tied to it with rope.

Help was summoned and the body was carried to Lymm's nearby Bull's Head Inn, where it was examined by Dr. Thomas Grundy, a local surgeon.

The girl wore a red and white bedgown, a pair of stays, a black skirt, white underskirt, a calico shift and coarse black stockings. She had neither hat nor shoes. One of her pockets contained a red ribbon and a penny, but there was no clue to her identity.

From bruises on her arms and back, the doctor concluded that the girl had been kicked and beaten before her neck was broken, killing her instantly. News of the find soon reached Manchester, and a few hours later a distraught Mrs. Eckersley identified the body as that of her missing daughter.

The following day an inquest was held at the Bull's Head Inn. Evidence was given that Tom Done had often threatened Betty, and had carried her off against her will on the night she was last seen alive. The court heard that his boat had passed through Lymm only a week before, and the jury returned a verdict of murder, naming Tom Done as the killer.

Betty was buried in Lymm churchyard the same day, and the authorities began to look for Done.

By September 8th he had been arrested and was in prison. "I am innocent of the death of Betty Eckersley," he protested.

Robert Holroyd, who had also been arrested, at first claimed he knew nothing, saying he had met Betty for the first time during the Sunday evening drinking session at the Bull's Head in Manchester. He had drunk so much that he could remember little of what happened after he left the pub, except that he had managed to get back to the boat and his bed.

He couldn't recall seeing Done bring Betty on board, he said, but when he went into the captain's cabin the next morning he had found the girl sitting there. He hadn't been surprised as he knew that she and Done had been close in the past.

After the barge had passed through Castlefield — a loading and unloading centre for boats in the heart of Manchester — and had joined the Bridgewater Canal he went into the cabin again and found it empty. As he hadn't seen Betty disembark, he wondered what had become of her.

Done told him he had put her ashore at Oxford Road while Holroyd had been busy. Later, at 2.30 p.m., while the *Six Brothers* was passing through Cornbrook on the outskirts of Manchester, a woman put her head through the cabin-hatch of a passing boat. Holroyd said he was surprised to see it was Miss Eckersley.

At 7 p.m. the barge reached Lymm, where Done decided to stop for the night. At about five o'clock the next morning they set off on the last leg of their journey to Runcorn. Holroyd swore he had neither seen nor heard anything out of the ordinary during the entire trip.

Then on September 9th, the day after making this statement, Holroyd changed his story. Perhaps he had heard that the case against Done was strengthening and feared that if he didn't tell all he knew, he might be charged with complicity.

Whatever the reason, Holroyd now said that on the morning the *Six Brothers* set out from Manchester for Runcorn he had seen Betty in Done's cabin, apparently in good health.

At this point, Holroyd said, he left the boat to fetch the horse from where it had been stabled overnight. When he returned an hour later Done had unloaded the vessel. The horse was then harnessed and the boat set off for Castlefield, where it would take on a fresh cargo. But with many boats loading and unloading and negotiating locks, delays were inevitable and progress was slow.

By mid-morning they had still not left Manchester. Irritated by the delays, Done left the boat which was now waiting in a long queue to pass through a lock. He told

Holroyd he was going for a drink at the Woodman in nearby Piccadilly.

Holroyd said he was busying himself about the boat when he spotted an old friend, Tom Chadwick, on another barge. He shouted to him, inviting him to come on board for a glass of rum. This was kept in Done's cabin, and the two went down to find it.

It was about noon, and on going inside they saw Betty lying on Done's bed. When she didn't respond to her name Chadwick touched her hand, which was cold. On closer inspection, Holroyd continued, he saw that her face and the side of her neck were "as black as my hat." She was obviously dead.

He and Chadwick left the cabin at once. As he hurriedly went back to his own boat, Chadwick said only that it was "a great pity."

Holroyd said he ran to the Woodman, where he found Done drinking with a couple of friends. "Come, Tom, let's go," he urged him. He said nothing about finding the girl's body, he claimed, because he feared he might be blamed for her death. He decided it would be better if Done himself discovered it.

As they neared Oxford Road, Done finally went below. When he returned ashen-faced, he said: "This woman is dead, we must keep our own counsel, or we shall both be hanged."

In his statement Holroyd said he himself began to cry, swearing he wasn't responsible and adding that Tom Chadwick had also seen the body. Done made no comment, and nothing further was said until they were approaching Lymm. Done then announced that he had put the body into a sack.

When they arrived at Lymm, Holroyd continued, he went about his duties as if nothing had happened. Leaving Done on the boat, he took the horse to be stabled overnight at the Bull's Head Inn. After paying the landlord John Wrigley the 1s. 8d. stabling fee, he decided to have a few drinks before he returned to the barge.

Although it was only nine o'clock when he got back, he found that Done had gone to bed. The captain didn't stir again, Holroyd insisted. He was sure about that because he had been so disturbed by the day's events that he hadn't slept at all himself and would have heard any movement.

Early the next morning the boat continued to Runcorn, Done's home-town and the end of their journey. On arriving, Done again said that they must keep their own counsel or they would hang.

On September 2nd the *Six Brothers* had arrived back in Manchester. Throughout the trip Done said nothing about Betty. Holroyd, unable to stand it any longer, demanded to know what the captain had done with her body. Done refused to tell him, saying that if the mate didn't want "to swing" they must tell anyone who asked about the girl that she left the barge at Oxford Road and they last saw her in a boat at Cornbrook.

Holroyd, out of fear for his life, had initially gone along with this. But now, as well as making his second statement, he identified the rope found tied to the body as having come from Done's boat. He recognised it, he said, because of the way it was "whipped at the ends."

On hearing of his first mate's new statement, Done made one himself. He said he had helped Holroyd dispose of Betty's body, but he didn't suggest the Yorkshireman was the killer.

"On leaving the Bull's Head on the evening of Sunday, August 27th, Miss Eckersley agreed to come back with me to the boat and stayed the night," his statement began. "At seven o'clock the next morning I gave her a glass of rum and put the bottle back in the cupboard. I then went up on deck to start the day's work, leaving her below alive and hearty. I did not see her again until we reached Oxford Road.

"I went into the cabin and found her lying on the bed, dead. Her knees were drawn towards her face and her face was bent towards her knees."

Done went on to say that he hurried back on deck and

found Holroyd, who was on the towpath attending to the horse. He told him that Betty was dead and asked him if he knew what had killed her. Holroyd said he didn't know, but when Done mentioned that some of his rum was missing, the mate suggested Betty might have drunk herself to death.

Fearing that he might be charged with murder if the corpse was found on his boat, Done said he pondered what to do next. "As we neared Lymm, Holroyd proposed she should be put into a sack and thrown into the River Bollin, which runs close to the village."

Done said he objected to this, saying, "No, she shall be put into the canal where she may be found and get interred."

He took a large stone from the canal bank and tied it to the sack containing Betty's body, which he then threw overboard with Holroyd's help. He speculated that the corpse had subsequently been struck by passing boats — hence the bruises and broken neck.

Done stuck to this story right to the end, but it conflicted with Holroyd's account. So who was telling the truth?

The authorities located Tom Chadwick, who Holroyd claimed was with him when he discovered Betty's body.

On September 14th Chadwick admitted seeing a woman lying on a bed in Done's cabin at around noon on August 28th. He remembered accidentally brushing against her hand as it hung over the side of the bunk.

"I looked upon the bed," he recalled, "and saw the face of a woman which was very pale and which shocked me."

He said he had turned to Holroyd and asked, "What does the woman ail from, do you think, Robert?" Holroyd said he didn't know.

Suspecting she was drunk, Chadwick said he asked if Done had given the girl anything to drink. Holroyd replied that he thought he had, but did not elaborate.

Chadwick went on to say that on returning to his own boat he told his wife of the young woman lying in Done's cabin who looked so sick that he had been frightened. But he told no-one else.

He denied telling Holroyd the girl was dead and remarking that it was a great pity.

But was he claiming Betty was alive because he felt guilty about reporting a possible murder?

Two more witnesses then came forward, however, with information which supported Chadwick's statement that Betty was still alive at a time when both Done and Holroyd insisted she was dead. It seemed that she might well have been living when the barge reached Lymm that evening.

John Wrigley, the landlord of the Bull's Head at Lymm, had been in his back yard at around midnight on August 28th when he heard a woman's agonising cries coming from the direction of the canal where the *Six Brothers* was moored.

"Lord Jesus! Oh, my God!" were the words he heard — "As if in the last extremity," he was later to say. As he listened the woman screamed again, but this time her voice was weaker and he was unable to make out the words. He assumed that a woman was in labour and thought no more about it, until Betty's body was discovered.

His neighbour Mrs. Middlebrook, though unsure of the date, also recalled hearing screams at around midnight. The cries sounded like "the voice of a woman in great distress."

Had Betty been drugged and then murdered as she tried to escape from the boat where she had been kept prisoner by Done, possibly with Holroyd's connivance? It was known that both men were on the barge when Wrigley heard the screams, and both were charged with Betty's murder.

They pleaded not guilty when their trial began at Chester Assizes on Monday, April 30th, 1810, before Sir Robert Dallas.

Robert Holroyd was acquitted, but Tom Done was convicted and sentenced to death after the jury heard how he had carried Betty onto his boat against her will. The court was also told that in the past he had threatened her: "I will be an enemy to you by night and by day for having kept company with another man."

Described in a newspaper report as "a resigned and devout penitent," Tom Done was hanged on Wednesday, May 2nd, 1810, at the new city gaol.

Earlier that morning at Chester Castle, where he had been held since his arrest, he insisted that although he had put Betty in the sack and had thrown her in the canal, she had died of natural causes.

After his execution his body was cut down and sent to the city hospital for dissection, the customary practice at that time.

Just where and when Betty Eckersley was murdered, between one Bull's Head and another, was to remain a mystery forever.

2
THE INFATUATION OF WALTER CHIPPERFIELD

"Sincerely, you are the only love there has ever been in all my life"

SHE WAS 30. He was 60. But Walter Chipperfield did not see this age gap as a hindrance to romance. A romance which had begun, at least for him, in the summer of 1928. Newly widowed, he had taken his nine-year-old son on holiday to Whitby in Yorkshire. Staying at the same hotel were the Richardson family from Gatley in Cheshire: John Richardson, a retired police sergeant, his wife and their two grown-up children, John and Edith.

Walter, a quiet man feeling lonely since his wife's death, was at once captivated by Edith. She was tall, athletically built and had a bright extovert personality. Pretending friendship with her father, a man his own age, Walter sought her out at every opportunity.

Being a caring person, Edith was sympathetic when she heard of his recent bereavement and did her best to cheer him up. She accepted his invitation to accompany him and his son on their sightseeing trips around town. As they strolled together along the harbour and through the winding streets, they talked. He about his life in London, where he worked as the manager of a transport company. She about her love of tennis, dancing and music — she was an accomplished pianist. But in case she sounded too frivolous, she added that she was also a Sunday school teacher and a church worker.

The two hit it off so well that Edith asked him to call her "Pat," as all her friends did. He told her to call him Walter. But because she didn't care for the name and thought "Mr. Chipperfield" too formal, she asked if he'd mind her calling him just "Chips."

Walter was delighted. He was in love with her, and although she was half his age he hoped she might feel the same way about him. But each time he tried to take her arm or hold her hand she would politely but firmly pull away.

At the end of the holiday, at his insistence, they exchanged addresses. But a postal relationship for a man who felt as strongly as he did inevitably proved unsatisfactory. To the amazement of his family and friends, he left his job in London and took up an appointment with Craven Brothers, an engineering company in Stockport ... just a few miles from Gatley, where Edith lived.

Having made this move, Walter must have been disappointed by the less than warm reception Edith gave him when he turned up unannounced at her parents' cottage. Unwilling to hurt anyone's feelings if she could avoid it, however, once she recovered from her initial shock she made him welcome. Later, she took him around the village and introduced him to her friends. They found him kind and affable, but were surprised at how old he was — too old for Edith, they thought, though it was obvious that he was in love with her.

Edith still made it clear she did not return his affection, but Walter persevered. Would she like him to teach her to drive in his new two-seater coupé? Desperate to learn, she couldn't resist the offer.

Each evening, after she had finished her work as a ledger clerk in Manchester, Walter drove around to her home to collect her. But he rarely went inside: her parents strongly objected to their daughter going out with a man so much older than herself.

It was during one of the lessons that Walter begged

Edith to marry him, telling her: "Sincerely, you are the only love there has ever been in all my life."

Deeply embarrassed, Edith told him that though she was extremely flattered she could not accept because she didn't feel as he did.

But Walter wouldn't take no for an answer, no matter how many times and in how many ways it was said. From then on each time they met he would plead with her to change her mind. At last, worn down by his insistence and not wanting to hurt his feelings, she reluctantly agreed.

Walter was overjoyed and the next evening presented her with an expensive five-stone diamond ring. For a while this relieved the pressure as they settled down to what turned out to be a very long engagement. But after three years Walter began pressing his fiancée to name the day.

She kept putting it off. First it was going to be Whitweek, then August. Then, realising she could never marry a man she didn't love, much to the relief of her family Edith broke off the engagement.

Walter, tears streaming down his cheeks, implored her not to stop seeing him completely, saying she was his only friend in Cheshire. Taking pity on him yet again, Edth agreed to see him once a week. But only, she stressed, as a friend. A releived Walter asked her to keep the ring as a token of their friendship.

He now went to Gatley every Thursday evening to see her. They would go out for a drive or just sit and talk in the cottage. But it soon became clear that Walter still hoped Edith would change her mind and marry him. In August, 1932, her mother wrote him a letter. Exasperated by the effect his persistence was having on Edith's health, she told Walter that it was hopeless for him to "cherish any idea of marriage with my daughter." But he wrote back beseeching her to allow the friendship to continue. He simply would not be rebuffed.

It wasn't only in Walter's private life that things were going wrong. He had given up his position with Craven Brothers and had bought a café in Bramhall, a few miles from Gatley. He had also sold his house and he and his son now lived in cramped rooms above the café.

Trade wasn't good and he was soon in debt. The effect of this additional worry was disastrous. Gone was the mild-mannered, easy-going Walter; now he seemed to be constantly in a bad temper. He told his son that if things got any worse he would shoot himself, a threat the boy took seriously because he knew his father still had his old army revolver.

So matters drifted until the summer of 1933. For five long years Edith had wanted to break with Walter for good, but had hesitated, fearful of the pain she would cause him. But on Wednesday, June 14th, she grasped the nettle at last and wrote to him ending their relationship for ever and returning his ring.

"You must understand by now what my feelings are," she concluded. She posted the letter that night and Walter received it at the café the following morning. But he showed no sign of the devastating news he had received. In fact, he seemed to be in a very good mood. When his son asked if he would go to the cinema that evening he cheerily agreed, warned him not to stay out too late and gave him two shillings.

Meanwhile, at work in Manchester, Edith was worried. How would "Chips" react to her letter? She told a colleague that she was terrified by the thought of returning to Gatley that evening. When her train arrived at Gatley station at 6.20 p.m., she saw Walter waiting in his car. He got out and politely offered her a lift. Perhaps in order to avoid a scene in front of other people, she accepted.

A few minutes later Sam Higgins was driving down Stone Pail Road, Gatley, when he saw a small car racing towards him. He sounded his horn frantically, but the other car continued to come straight at him. As he screeched to a halt, the other car passed so closely that their mudguards touched. And to his horror Higgins saw the man at the wheel point a gun at the woman beside him and shoot her. She screamed and the car drove on down

Stone Pail Road.

Mrs. Dorothy Jackson, wife of the village newsagent, was walking down the street when she saw the two cars almost collide. As Higgins's car came to a halt the other swerved past him and sped on towards her. As it did she heard shots and a woman screaming, "He's shooting me! He's shooting me!"

Then the car slowed, the door was flung open and Edith Richardson leapt out. As she did so a man leaned out of the car and continued shooting at her as she cowered in terror.

Despite the danger, Mrs Jackson dashed towards Edith, and as the bullets whistled about her she lifted the wounded girl's head and cradled it in her lap. Covered in blood and groaning, Edith died a few moments later.

Hearing the shots, others came running from nearby houses. When they saw Edith lying in the road they thought she had been the victim of a car accident. They couldn't believe it when they learned that she had been gunned down in the middle of their peaceful village.

Meanwhile Sam Higgins had got out of his car and was running down the road, hoping to stop the killer escaping. Instead of speeding off, the assailant's car had run into a hedge, swung into the centre of the road and come to a standstill.

Knowing the man was armed, Higgins approached the car cautiously. As he did so he heard three more shots, and through the windscreen he saw the driver's head jerk back and then slump forward over the wheel. Opening the car door, Higgins saw blood gushing from the man's gaping mouth.

Walter Chipperfield was dead. When his pockets were later searched by the police they found Edith's engagement ring together with a long letter he had addressed to her, but never posted, urging her not to end their relationship. They also found Edith's letter, to which Walter had added a postscript saying that he now realised there was nothing more to be done.

During the shooting, Edith's brother had been standing at the front door of the family home on Gatley Green, but had heard nothing.

He only learned of the tragedy when his fiancée brought him the news and he had the task of telling his parents.

Hurrying to the scene, the family were distressed to find Edith's body still lying in the road. They asked for it to be removed, but to their astonishment they were told that this was impossible at the moment. Edith had been murdered at the spot on the road which marked the boundary between the City of Manchester and Cheshire, and the two police forces were disputing which had jurisdiction. So the bullet-riddled body lay in the road for more than an hour before the matter was resolved and the Manchester police had both corpses taken to a mortuary.

Meanwhile, Chipperfield's 14-year-old son was told in the foyer of a Stockport cinema that his father was dead and he was needed to identify the body. As he wiped his tears away, he told the police that though he knew his father was fond of Miss Richardson and they had quarrelled a lot, he never thought it would lead to murder.

At the inquest into the deaths, held in Manchester on June 19th, Dr. H. F. Scotson said he had found six bullets in Edith, two of which had gone through her heart. In Chipperfield's case, two bullets had entered his chest and death was due to a ruptured aorta. The weapon used was produced. It was an automatic revolver capable of firing nine shots, which Chipperfield's son identified as having belonged to his father.

One by one, Edith's friends told the court the same tragic story.

"I think," said one, "that she had always been perfectly honest with Mr. Chipperfield and had given him to understand that though she had a great respect for him she could not profess to love him ... But then she felt she must end their relationship for good, if she was to be honest with herself and with Mr. Chipperfield. For a long time she wondered how she could break the news of her decision. It was only on Wednesday that she made up her mind to write the letter and return the ring."

The coroner, Mr. C. W. C. Surridge, told the jury: "Your verdict in this case can only be one of murder in the case of the man."

Referring to the state of Chipperfield's mind, he went on: "He threatened to take his life six months ago, owing to business depression. There is no real evidence of what you would call insanity."

The jury duly brought in the recommended verdict.

That night Edith's body lay in Gatley Church, and the following morning the whole village turned out to attend her funeral. Everyone agreed that she was the last person they thought would ever have been murdered. Ironically, if she hadn't been so soft-hearted the romance that never was would not have obsessed the infatuated Walter Chipperfield. She would still have been alive ... and so would he.

3
WHO BURNED BABY HELEN?

A story from Blackburn that will shock and mystify

MOST FOLK in the Lancashire town of Blackburn were enjoying their last few hours of leisure on Sunday, June 30th, 1935, before the working week began again the following morning. But it was a different scene in John Bright Street, where the worried residents roamed the neighbourhood. Three-year-old Helen, the only child of Mr. and Mrs. Charles Chester, had disappeared.

When she was last seen by her mother, Helen had been playing happily not far from her home, 22 John Bright Street. But when Mrs. Chester went to call her in five minutes later there was no sign of her.

The police were called and promptly began searching local warehouses, workshops and empty buildings. Then it was established that Helen had last been seen crossing a footbridge which spanned the nearby River Darwen. Fearing that she had fallen into the water and drowned, officers patrolled the river banks throughout the night but there was no trace of Helen.

At 9 p.m. Mr. Fred Pickering, who also lived in John Bright Street, became concerned about his own daughter, five-year-old Margaret, and went out to look for her. When he couldn't find her in the street he called at No. 24, the house next door to that of the Chesters.

This was the home of an elderly couple, James and Edith Mills. They were both fond of children, and

Margaret, like most of the other youngsters in the street, was always made welcome and given little treats like biscuits. Pickering found Jim Mills standing at his door and asked him if his daughter was in the house.

"Margaret's wanted!" the old man shouted into the kitchen. A moment later, a bright-eyed little girl bounced happily out of the house and into her father's arms. Pickering gave her a good telling-off for staying out so late. The police later questioned her; but she hadn't seen Helen since that afternoon.

The search for the missing girl continued and early on Monday morning the police announced that if she weren't found soon they would search every house in John Bright Street.

At 3 p.m. that Monday afternoon Henry Ball was surprised to see a sudden cloud of black smoke, mingled with what appeared to be pieces of burning paper, pour from Jim Mills's chimney. The smoke continued to belch from the chimney for two minutes and then stopped as abruptly as it had appeared. Ball assumed the old couple were burning rubbish. Meanwhile the search for Helen continued.

At 6.45 a.m. on Tuesday Thomas Farnworth and his wife, who lived two doors down from the Chesters, were getting up for work. As Mrs. Farnworth went downstairs to the kitchen to prepare breakfast she glanced through the window and saw a large parcel lying by the back door. She called to her husband, who was certain there had been nothing in the yard when he locked up at 10.45 the previous evening.

Going outside he found the yard door still firmly barred. The parcel was wrapped in newspaper. Undoing the cord which secured it, he parted the paper and found half a bed-quilt.

As he shook the material something tumbled out which would haunt him for the rest of his life. It was the charred body of a young child, so badly burnt that it at first appeared to be little more than a mass of cinders.

Both arms were missing and the legs had been burnt away leaving just two blackened stumps about two inches long. Stumbling to his feet, Tom Farnworth hurried to fetch the police.

As officers gathered around to examine the gruesome find, the Farnworths' next door neighbour Jim Mills came to his side of the yard wall. Popping his head over, he said, "I was looking out of the bedroom window at five o'clock this morning and I saw a parcel there."

Asked why he hadn't informed anyone, he replied, "I didn't know it was the child."

Neither the police nor Farnworth had told anyone of what had been found, so how could Mills have known what was in the parcel unless it was he who put it there?

An hour later the Chief Constable of Blackburn, Mr. C. G. Looms, Superintendent Langley, Dr. Bailey the police surgeon, and other officers went to Mills's home.

"I hear you saw a parcel at five o'clock today," Looms told him.

"Yes," replied Mills, saying he had been up early because he had been worrying about Helen and couldn't sleep. He then took Looms upstairs and showed him the spot through his bedroom window from which he claimed to have seen the parcel. But when Looms stood in the same position he found it impossible to see all of that spot. Seeing it would have required more than a casual glance. The Chief Constable then wanted to know why Mills had not reported it to the police.

Mills shrugged and said again, "I didn't know it was the child."

"Nobody has said that it is," replied Looms.

Mills shifted uneasily. "Well, they've been talking about it around here this morning," he said.

Returning downstairs to the kitchen, Looms studied the roaring fire. Around the grate were signs that it had recently been cleaned, as it was damp. Questioned about this, Mills insisted that the grate hadn't been cleaned for a long time, saying it was damp because his wife had taken a bath in the kitchen the previous day.

One of the officers then put the fire out. Traces of a greasy substance, possibly animal fat, could now be seen around the inside of the grate, and there was a strong smell of burnt flesh. The policeman began poking around in the ashpan and soon discovered four pieces of charred bone, which Dr. Bailey identified as human.

There were also some metal buttons similar to the ones on the navy blue blazer Helen had been wearing.

Questioned about the bones found in his grate, Mills replied: "Bones? Oh yes! We had breast of mutton yesterday and I threw the bones on the fire." When it was pointed out that they were not mutton bones he said, "Oh, I remember now, the cat brought a stinking fish head in and the missus threw it on the fire."

In the kitchen sink police discovered a piece of bone, and charred substances were retrieved from the wastepipe. In Mills's bedroom — he and his wife had separate rooms — detectives found bloodstains on the quilt. Looms also noticed that the floor had been recently scrubbed and newspaper placed over it. Mills explained that his wife had asked him to clean his bedroom floor. That was why, he now claimed, he had been up at five o'clock — to make an early start on the chore.

The police also found a screwed-up piece of bloodstained newspaper with a long blonde hair attached to it. When this was shown to Mills he said the hair was probably his wife's; but her hair was grey. It was Helen's that was blonde.

In Mrs. Mills's bedroom detectives found the other half of the quilt which had been wrapped around the child's body. Hidden beneath clothing at the bottom of a drawer were several fragments of charred bone, one of which Dr. Bailey immediately identified as a piece of human thigh-bone.

Mrs. Mills had no explanation for the bones or how they came to be in her room. Of the quilt she said, "A good while ago it was torn in half and half was used as an ironing cloth." But on closer examination it showed signs of having only recently been torn in two. Asked where the other half was now she insisted it was in the kitchen, but the police couldn't find it.

The body had been wrapped in pages nine and ten of a Sunday newspaper, a copy of which was found in the house with those two pages missing. The length of cord used to tie up the parcel was similar to a piece of old clothes-line fastened to an outhouse in the yard.

In the outside toilet the police found a silver-coloured chain which Mr. Chester had earlier described as having been given to Helen to play with on the evening she disappeared. Detectives also discovered charred paper and a piece of clothing on the wall which divided the Millses' and Farnworths' backyards. From this it was apparent that Helen's body had been pushed over the wall from the Millses' side.

When told of this Mills claimed that someone had come into his yard during the night, saying that when he came down that morning he had found the door unbolted. But the police found that it would have been impossible to have unbolted the door from the other side. When this was pointed out Mills said that it could be undone with a piece of wire, but no wire was found.

"I know nowt about it," was Mills's only comment when he was arrested and taken to Blackburn police station.

There he said that on the evening of Helen's disappearance he had gone to visit a cousin who lived in Coniston Road, on the other side of Blackburn, and had not left her house until 7.45. This meant that he would not have arrived home until 8.15. Mrs. Mills claimed it was 8.30 when he returned, while he said it was nearer 8.45, as he had taken the route through the market place where he paused to hear a local politician making a speech.

When he arrived home, he said, he found Margaret Pickering playing there. He had not seen Helen Chester. His account of his movements was checked and found to be correct.

Meanwhile, back in John Bright Street, Mrs. Mills was making a statement to Superintendent Langley:

"On Sunday my husband and I had tea at 5 p.m. After that I cleared the table and sat reading. At 7 p.m. he asked if I was going for a walk and I said, 'No, I am going to read.' He then left the house by the back door and he came in the same way at about 8.30 p.m. A little girl named Margaret Pickering came to the front door at about 7.45 p.m., and running into the front room told me, 'Helen Chester is lost,' and that was the first I had heard of her being missing. We then all had a little supper. At 9 p.m. Margaret's father came for her."

According to Mrs. Mills, the couple then went to bed, but she found she couldn't sleep and went into the back bedroom to talk to her husband who was also still awake. "My word, it must be serious about Helen," she said, going to the window and peering out. "The houses are lit up at the back and men have been out with lanterns."

"She'll be in someone's house," he replied, turning over and closing his eyes. Mrs. Mills was struck by his apparent lack of concern. "Do you think you should get up?

"It looks bad you laid there and all the men in the street have been out with lanterns," she told him. But he did not get up and she returned to bed. She still couldn't sleep and she kept getting up to look out of the window. Both she and her husband rose at 6 a.m. and after breakfast they sat in the kitchen talking about the child's disappearance.

Mrs. Mills continued: "We had dinner of cabbage and breast of mutton. Afterwards my husband washed the dinner pots and I told him I would have a bath. He then lit the fire under the boiler to heat the water. While I washed, my husband left the house by the back way and did not return until between four and five o'clock.

"A short time earlier an old lady, Mrs. Cooper, popped her head in and said, 'They are dragging the brook for little Helen.' I put on my shawl and went to look. I stayed at the brook-side for about half an hour. On getting home my husband was making tea. I said to him, 'Have you been then at the brook?' and he said, 'No, I have been the other way by the laundry looking for little Helen.'

Apart from her husband going out for a loaf, neither of them left the house again that evening she said. They then went to bed. When she rose at about 7.30 a.m. she found her husband was up already.

"He had lit the fire and had made my breakfast ready," she told Langley. "On going downstairs he said, 'They are finding little Helen. She is in the next yard, I think.' I asked him if someone had told him and he said, 'No, but the police are in the next yard. I think they have found her body.'

"My husband told me that someone had been in our yard because when he went to bed he had bolted the backyard door, and when he got up that morning the door was unfastened. He also told me that he had heard a noise about five o'clock."

As Mrs. Mills was stone deaf, in order to read back her statement to her Langley had to shout directly into her ear. Then she was taken to Blackburn police station.

At the mortuary Professor J. E. W. MacFall, Professor of Forensic Medicine at Liverpool University, assisted by Dr. Bailey, carried out a post-mortem examination. They found that Helen had died as the result of shock caused by a single heavy blow to the top of her head, which could have been delivered by a hammer. The hole in her skull was of about the same span as the head of a hammer found in Mills's cellar.

The professor thought it most unlikely that the injury had been caused accidentally. Helen would have been dead when the attempt was made to burn her body. The bones found were identical with those of a child of three, and the thigh-bone found in Mrs. Mills's bedroom drawer fitted precisely into the socket on the corpse.

All the bloodstains discovered in the house were human, and a lock of Helen's hair which her mother had cut as a keepsake on the child's third birthday was compared to the hair remaining on the body and found to be almost an exact match.

Mr. Chester had never once doubted that the remains were his daughter's. There was the piece of polished chain which the child had used as a toy. "I polished it for her," he told reporters, "as she liked to play with it. It was a little piece of bridle chain. I should have identified it anywhere. Helen was a bright child, just beginning to talk nicely to us, and so happy and cheerful when she was playing out on Sunday night. We searched all over and I have not slept at all, except for a couple of hours this morning, since she disappeared. The police told us early this morning about finding the body. There is no doubt at all, it is Helen's."

When both Mr. and Mrs. Mills were charged with the murder, Mills told his wife: "Don't say a word." And she didn't.

Neighbours were incredulous when they heard that the two had been arrested. How could such a nice old couple who obviously adored children have come to murder one?

Then rumours began to circulate that Jim Mills had held a grudge against Charles Chester, who was a drapery salesman. William Clegg told of a conversation he had had in his shop with Mills the day before Helen's body was found. Mills had said that the child had not drowned in the River Darwen, as was then speculated, because there wasn't enough water. In his opinion she had been playing by the brook-side and on running out had got knocked down by a car. Panicking, the driver had put her body in the vehicle and taken it away to dump it elsewhere.

Mills had added that he thought Chester would take it badly — "He's a weakling and should have been nursed, not wedded."

But Chester told the police that he'd had no quarrel with Mills, although he felt that Mills didn't like him. "I was not unfriendly with Mr. Mills," he said of the man who had been his neighbour for 20 years, "but had no conversation with him. He did not look pleasant when passing me and I got out of the way. But I did not have any ill-feeling towards him."

The murder trial of James and Edith Mills, both aged 62, began at Lancaster Castle on October 16th, 1935. Mills appeared in a blue suit and his wife wore a small black hat and brown coat with a fur collar. Both pleaded "not guilty."

Many grotesque exhibits, including photographs of the dead child's mutilated body, were provided for the jury's scrutiny. But one picture was thought too distressing by the judge and was not shown to them.

The defence offered no evidence and neither Mills nor his wife entered the witness box.

Mr. Jackson KC, prosecuting, maintained that Helen had died violently at the hands of one of the accused while in the other's presence. The couple had then attempted to dispose of the body by burning it on their kitchen fire. Fearing, however, that the black smoke would attract attention, they had decided instead to parcel Helen like laundry and leave her remains in a neighbour's backyard.

He dismissed the defence's argument that Helen's death had been accidental. If they were so sure of this, why hadn't they produced any medical evidence? And why hadn't the defendants, in the 14 weeks since their arrest, pleaded it was so and explained what had happened?

"If it were an accident what was there to hide?" asked the prosecutor. "Why should grown-up people go through that terrible, revolting, ghoulish act [burning the body] unless there was something of a terrible nature which they wished to hide?"

Mr. W. Gorman KC, defending Mills, did not dispute that the couple had tried to dispose of Helen's body, but he maintained that her death had been accidental.

Referring to the prosecution's claim that putting the body on the fire had been the act of murderers, Mr. Gorman asked the jury: "Have you any right to say that? Are you satisfied that it was not the act of a person demented and distraught, the death of a child having taken place in circumstances which might attach blame to that person?"

Mr. Gorman went on to claim that Mills was not even in the house when the incident, whether accident or murder, had taken place.

Defending Mrs. Mills, Mr. Glynne Blackledge also argued that Helen's death was accidental, pointing out that in the Millses' house there was furniture on which a child might climb and fall and a dark staircase with 13 steps.

Mr. Justice Hilbery, summing-up, accepted that Helen's death might have been accidental, but said he thought it strange that if this were the case an "innocent person" had not simply gone to get help. The judge also observed that carbolic soap had been found in the couple's kitchen.

Quoting Shakespeare, he commented that whoever had taken the body from the fire would have needed something as strong as carbolic soap "to wash this filthy witness from our hands." But to convict the couple, he warned the jury, they must look for evidence of murder, not just the burning of the body.

After deliberating for two hours the jury found both Mills and his wife guilty, but made a recommendation for mercy in the case of Mrs. Mills.

Asked if he had anything to say before the death sentence was passed, Jim Mills replied in a voice barely above a whisper: "I am absolutely innocent, sir, that is all I have to say." Mrs. Mills, remained silent.

It was the first case for nearly a century in which a husband and wife had been convicted of murder and sentenced to death. Without being allowed a moment together in private the couple were taken to separate prisons, Mills to Walton Gaol in Liverpool, his wife to Strangeways in Manchester.

When the couple's appeal was heard on November 21st, 1935, Mr. Gorman said that Mills wished to appear as a witness, his plea now being that he did not give evidence at the trial because he had not wanted to incriminate his wife.

His application was refused, but he was allowed to have

a written statement read to the court. "I was not guilty," it began. "I was not in the house at any material time." He explained that not only was he away from his home when Helen Chester disappeared, but he was also absent from it at 3 o'clock on Monday afternoon when smoke and burnt paper was seen coming from his chimney.

Saying that he had not come home on that Monday until 5 p.m., he hinted that his wife was in a poor mental state and said he had heard her go downstairs and into the backyard on the night before Helen's body was discovered. He denied he had ever seen or touched the corpse.

Other grounds for the appeal centred on the judge's summing-up. Mr. Gorman argued that Mr. Justice Hilbery had failed to point out that Helen could have been murdered before Mills returned home, and if this were so he was only guilty of aiding and abetting his wife in the disposal of the body.

The appeal judges consisting of Lord Justices Goddard, MacNaghten and Atkinson accepted that Mills was nowhere near John Bright Street at the time Helen Chester disappeared. On his return Margaret Pickering had been in the house and had remained there until 9 p.m. This meant that had he murdered Helen she would have had to have remained hidden in the house for an hour and a quarter and the judges found this "highly improbable."

They also accepted that the trial judge had not informed the jury of other verdicts they could reach in Mills's case if they accepted that Helen Chester had been killed on first entering the house when he could not have been there. On these grounds the court decided that Mills's conviction must be quashed.

But the judges found that Mrs. Mills must have been in the house when Helen was murdered, and her appeal was dismissed. As judgement was given she sat meekly with her hands clasped in front of her, unable to hear and not moving until a wardress touched her on the shoulder. She then rose mechanically from her seat and walked slowly from the dock.

However, her case was later reviewed by the Home Secretary and she was reprieved on November 27th.

Just how Helen Chester came to die remained a mystery, as did the extent of Mills's involvement. Even if he took no part in the disposal of the body, it seems that at the least he tried to cover up for his wife, and walked free because he had been charged only with murder.

4
THE GIRL FROM GALWAY

"I loved her and I am now here to die for her"

SITTING IN the condemned cell at Manchester's New
Bailey Prison, Timothy Faherty knew that within two
hours he would be swinging lifelessly from the end of a
rope. And all because of Mary Hanmer, the girl he had
loved too much. If only she had been more reasonable ...

His fists tightened at the memory of how she had
scorned and mocked him, and for a moment he again felt
the deadly rage which had driven him over the edge ...

Twenty-seven-year-old Timothy Faherty was the son of
a Galway farmer who had died during the boy's childhood.
After his mother's remarriage, Tim, unhappy with his
stepfather had left Ireland as soon as he was old enough to
fend for himself. Enlisting as a soldier, he had served in
India, Australia and New Zealand. Twelve years later he
left the army and went to live in Droylsden near
Manchester, where he had friends. He found work at
Hadwen & Ashworth's mill, and in August 1867 he went
to lodge with a widow, Mary Broaderick, in her small but
comfortable terraced house in Moorcroft Street.

The widow's other lodger was Mary Hanmer, a mill girl
who also came from Galway. Although she was nine years
Faherty's senior, her dark hair and flashing green eyes
made her an undeniable beauty and he swiftly fell under
her spell.

With Galway in common, they had much to talk about.

Mary told him that she had been sent to England as a child by her unmarried mother, who hoped that the stigma of bastardy would be less damning in a more liberal society.

Faherty easily forgave her that. He would have forgiven her anything. But Mary Hanmer was accustomed to dealing with lovesick men, and had the knack of being friendly and polite while keeping them all at arm's length. Her requirements in a serious suitor were very particular, and during her chats with Faherty she made no secret of what she sought in a husband. He had to be deeply pious, a devout Catholic, morally upstanding and a teetotaller. Faherty was determined to be all these.

Mary spoke of others who had tried to court her, and Faherty listened intently to the stories of those who had shown themselves to be woefully short of the qualities she required.

Tim Faherty was not a prude. Having been in the army he was fond of a drink once in a while, but if he had to convince Mary he was a total abstainer, so be it. He would withdraw from the pleasures of the alehouse and swear to her he had never tasted liquor.

Before long she was allowing him to accompany her to church. He had never before wanted to go to church so frequently, but he got precious little other encouragement to be with Mary. Kneeling beside her in prayer was therefore pure joy. Would she have been shocked had she known what Tim was praying for?

The sight of Mary Hanmer made abstinence from drink easy to bear, and Tim Faherty would gladly have sat looking at her for every minute of the day, had it been practicable. Work intruded, however, and his friends at the mill noted that he was the only man there who did not enjoy a drink now and again. So they decided to persuade him to have "just one." He didn't need much coaxing. "Just one" led to just another ... and then another until seven or eight pints later, Faherty realised he had a problem. How was he to sneak in at his lodgings without his landlady or Mary seeing what a state he was in?

At the front door the befuddled Tim Flaherty was under intense pressure to think. He had not only to get in, he had also to remember to be absolutely silent. He was not up to it. When the door closed behind him, he tried to propel himself forward without moving his feet — not as a matter of bravado but simple lack of concentration. Realising his error, as he fell he grabbed at the hallstand and took it down with him.

The thud, and the clattering as he extricated himself from the hats, coats, umbrellas and walking-sticks, woke up the entire household.

Mary and Mrs. Broaderick appeared at the top of the stairs, swathed in their dressing gowns. The light from their candles cast a halo around Mary's sweet face, making her look more like an angel than ever. But her expression was far from angelic.

Tim Faherty's blood froze. There was no getting out of this and he knew it. Who but a drunk would be crawling around on all fours at the bottom of the stairs, covered in coats and umbrellas?

Mary never again allowed him to escort her to church. With her there were no second chances; she said she could not bear to see him again. Tim left his lodgings and rented a room in a house in Rochdale Road. But he couldn't get Mary out of his mind, so he visited his old digs frequently.

She was always polite, but very distant. She made it quite clear that their relationship was finished. Tim would not and could not accept this. He thought that by persisting he could win her back. Rejection was turning his love into an obsession. Day by day, as Mary showed no signs of warming to him, he became increasingly frustrated.

On Christmas Eve, 1867, he visited Moorcroft Street and found Mrs. Broaderick and Mary putting up Christmas decorations. He asked them if they intended going to chapel at Gorton Friary to celebrate Midnight Mass. Mrs. Broaderick said she couldn't because she didn't have any silver. Tim looked hopefully at Mary. "Are you coming?" he asked.

She shook her head.

"Oh, come on, Mary, do come," he urged.

"But I shall have no-one to come home with me," she said, pinning up a spray of holly over the fireplace.

Tim laughed. "Don't be daft. I shall walk you home," he told her.

To his shock, Mary retorted, "Oh, I'd look very well, wouldn't I, coming home with a man at four o'clock in the morning?"

Her off-hand description of him as "a man" hurt Tim deeply, as perhaps it was meant to. He went to the door, and Mrs. Broaderick, seeing how upset he was, followed him out.

"Oh, cheer up, lad," she said. "After all, it is Christmas."

But Tim wouldn't be consoled. "I'm sorry I ever degraded myself so low as to once ask the question of a woman who promised me once and then denied me," he muttered angrily, before turning up his collar and hurrying away down the snow-covered street.

Mrs. Broaderick, sadly shaking her head, guessed that he had asked Mary to marry him and she had turned him down because of his drinking. The landlady wished he would forget Mary and find someone more amenable to love. After all, he was a good looking fellow. And Mary could be very wilful. Tim's wasn't the first heart she had broken.

On Christmas Day he paid Mary another visit at about three o'clock in the afternoon. Mrs. Broaderick was out, but her daughter Bridget was at home. She and Mary, having lived under the same roof for many years, thought of one another as sisters.

Bridget had been at Midnight Mass and had spotted Tim in the congregation, though they hadn't spoken. She supposed there was ill-feeling between him and Mary, so she was surprised to find him standing on the doorstep. She was even more surprised to see how cheerful he seemed to be. Then she smelt the alcohol on his breath as he entered the house.

Rubbing his hands in front of the blazing fire, he told Mary he would be going to Galway in the morning to see his mother, and asked if she had any messages for her folk. Mary shook her head. "No, I have no messages to send, but what I have, I have sent to my mother the week before last. But give my respects to the green fields of Ireland and the shamrock."

As Tim chatted about his mother, Mary began to clear the table and wash up the tea things. Bridget, tired after being so late for Midnight Mass the night before, excused herself and went upstairs for a nap.

While she was hanging her clothes on the rack above her fire to air, she heard something clatter in the kitchen below, and then Mary cry, "Oh, no, knives and forks are falling!"

Bridget knew that Mary thought this an evil omen. A moment later she heard Mary's voice again, shouting irritably, "Get off with you, why do you come in after me?"

Bridget assumed Tim had followed Mary into the kitchen and was trying to kiss her. She would have gone down to ensure that Tim didn't annoy Mary, but being exhausted she got into bed. In a minute she was fast asleep.

Nobody will ever know just what was said downstairs after Bridget dozed off. Perhaps Tim pleaded with Mary to marry him and she, smelling the drink on his breath, recoiled from his embrace. Perhaps Mary had flung some taunt at him. He was later to say she had called him a Protestant, saying that when he died she would see to it that he was buried in Droylsden's Protestant churchyard at St. Mary's, across the street from Moorcroft Road.

Whatever the provocation, he picked up the poker beside the fireplace and struck her over the head with it. Mary reeled backwards, screaming "Murder!" Then she ran for her life. Tim, with the poker still in his hand, was hard on her heels.

Bridget, woken by the scream, heard Mary's voice pleading piteously, "Don't, Tim, oh please don't."

Frightened, Bridget sprang out of bed and shut her bedroom door. But Mary, with all the strength of the dying, pushed it open and staggering inside crying out, "Bridget, Bridget, I am killed!"

Her hair was down and her face covered in blood. Tim came in behind her, shouting, "I will kill you! I will kill you!"

Raising the poker, he struck Mary on the back of the head. She did not move again, but Faherty frenziedly struck her five more blows.

Bridget could do little more than look on until the rage had abated. When the poker was raised a sixth time, it got caught up in the clothes on the rack and Bridget ran from the bedroom. She had reached the landing when she felt Tim's hands clasp her flowing hair. Screaming she broke free and leapt for the stairs.

Next door neighbour Thomas Brown was in the street outside when he heard the screams, and pushed his way into the house.

In the next instant Bridget hurled herself from the top of the stairs, giving Brown hardly time to brace himself to break her fall.

"Oh, he's killed my sister, Tim's killed my sister!" she sobbed.

Leaving Bridget in the care of another neighbour who had followed him in, Brown ran upstairs.

He found Tim, his clothes and hands covered in blood, on his knees in Bridget's bedroom beside Mary. Blood poured from Mary's smashed head, saturating everything around her. There was even blood on the ceiling.

"What the hell have you been doing?" Brown demanded.

"I gave her my honour and ... and ... I loved her and I am now here to die for her," Tim Faherty sobbed, caressing Mary's bloody face.

Brown's principal concern was the injured woman, who

was now gurgling. Realising that Faherty was so shocked that he presented no further danger, Brown fetched a glass of water from beside Bridget's bed and tried to get Mary to drink some, but it dribbled down her chin and onto her chest.

At 3.45 p.m. Police Constable George Lord was making his way along Market Street when he was stopped by a group of distraught women who told him there had been a murder in Moorcroft Street. Sending a boy to the police station to inform Inspector Harrop, Lord hurried to the address.

He arrived to find Faherty weeping over Mary, who was still alive but unable to speak. A doctor had been sent for, but Lord could see there was little hope.

Later, with Inspector Harrop, he traced the trail of blood through the scullery and parlour, up the stairs to Bridget's bedroom. After questioning Thomas Brown and Bridget, Harrop arrested Faherty and handcuffed him. As Lord led him away, Faherty indicated the poker at Mary's side and said, "Yes, that is it."

Although the poker was heavy, almost a yard long and an inch thick, it had completely buckled.

Tim tried to pull away from the policeman, leaning back to where Mary, had been propped, and whispering, "Oh, Mary, didn't I tell you ..."

Lord, however, would have no last-minute nonsense. Grabbing his prisoner by the collar and back of his trousers, he hauled him downstairs, shoved him through the crowd of onlookers clustered on the pavement, and threw him into the police van.

At the police station, Faherty was allowed to wash the blood off himself. As he was about to be searched, he said, "I've nothing upon me, for I was prepared for it." Constable Lord considered this a clear admission that the murder had been premeditated.

The surgeon, Robert Slater, arrived at the Moorcroft Street house at 4.15 p.m. Mary Hamner was unconscious. She hd lost so much blood that he could do no more for her than make her as comfortable as possible until she died at 5.11 p.m.

Harrop then charged Tim Faherty with Mary's murder. "Is she dead?" Faherty asked.

Told that she was, he replied in sudden anger, "The bitch accused me of being a bloody Protestant and said she would bury me in Droylsden's Protestant churchyard."

A few days later, two mothers set out from Galway for England to say goodbye for the last time to their children.

Mary Hanmer's destitute mother went to the Roman Catholic Church in Fairfield, near Droylsden, to attend the service for her daughter. She was so poor she had only a tattered handkerchief to cover her head in church. Her daughter's friends, moved to pity for the old lady, took up a collection for her with the result that when she returned to Ireland a few days later, she was better clothed and fed than she had ever been before.

Mrs. Faherty arrived in Droylsden on the same day as Mary's mother. Although she was neither as impoverished nor as alone — having her brother and two sisters with her — she was just as grief-stricken.

Throwing her arms around her son, in his cell, she cried, "Oh, Tim, my boy, I'm here!"

From that day on she visited him every Friday, but although she gave him comfort, her visits were also painful. He knew how much she was suffering to see him locked up for murder.

When his trial opened at Manchester Assizes on March 12th, 1868, he pleaded not guilty. He had now spent three months in prison, both cursing Mary and praying for her forgiveness. Now he cursed her again.

He displayed his only sign of remorse when Mrs. Broaderick was helped into the witness box. She was very old and the ordeal of appearing in court unnerved her to the point of collapse as she gave her evidence.

She found this so difficult, stumbling constantly over her words, that the judge lost patience and ordered her to be led out of court for some fresh air.

Mr. Ernest Jones, defending, accepted that Faherty had killed Mary Hanmer, but he questioned whether this had been premeditated. Had Faherty snatched up the poker in sudden anger, provoked by Mary calling him a Protestant?

The defence counsel also asked the jury to consider the influence of drink on Faherty that Christmas Day, and to take into account the long vigil of the Midnight Mass which Faherty had attended alone after being snubbed again by Mary. All these circumstances, Mr. Jones contended, made a strong case for the crime to be reduced from murder to manslaughter.

But Mr. Justice Lush told the jury, "If you believe the evidence, there are no circumstances in the case which could reduce the crime below that of murder. It might have been reduced to manslaughter if there was great provocation but there was nothing of that kind in this case. Words do not constitute that provocation. It is the clearest case of murder which could be conceived."

The jury found Timothy Faherty guilty, and he was sentenced to death.

His mother's visits were now doubly painful. He longed to touch her, to give her one final hug of farewell. But there could be no such contact between visitors and the condemned man, for the room was divided by a passage-way lined with iron bars and patrolled by a warder.

Faherty was hanged alongside the Todmorden murderer, Miles Weatherill, at 8 a.m. on Saturday, April 4th, 1868, and as this was known in advance to be the last public execution to take place in Lancashire, a larger than usual crowd was attracted. Hundreds massed outside the prison during the night to see the scaffold. Many had dispersed by 11 p.m., but the two condemned men endured the jeering of a group of 50 youths and their girls who at 3 a.m. began marching round the gaol singing "When Johnny Come Marching Home," and an obscene version of "Glory, Hallelujah."

Householders opposite the New Bailey let upstairs windows to those willing to pay for a good view, and hawkers prepared for a brisk trade in refreshments.

The crowd didn't hiss at Faherty as they did at Weatherill when the two condemned men took their places on the scaffold. Then the executioner, William Calcraft, did his duty and it was all over.

Perhaps, in a perverse way, Tim Faherty and Mary Hanmer had both achieved their ambitions. She had died pure, as she had wished, and he laid down his life for her ...

5
THE CONGLETON CANNIBAL

"God forbid!" screamed the woman. "He told me it was pork!"

H E WAS brutish-looking, in his mid-fifties, with dirty clothes and even dirtier hands. Most women would have been terrified at being accosted by such a man, especially on a secluded road at dusk. But 22-year-old Annie Smith was too poor and too hungry.

"Got any money?" she asked, noting the way the man's eyes explored her young body. "If thou hast" — she turned and with a suggestive smile gestured towards a nearby hollow — "perhaps we can have a little fun ..."

The man did not reply but followed her to the hollow. There, despite the November cold, she began to undo her bodice. Then she stopped and turning to the man she held out her hand, saying she wanted money before she went any further.

The man fumbled in his pockets. A moment later he brought something out which glinted like silver. It was not until Annie felt the excruciating pain in her stomach that she realised it wasn't a coin he had pulled from his pocket. It was a razor-sharp knife and the man was murdering her ...

It was noon on Saturday, November 23rd, 1776, when farmer Newman Garside decided to check his fencing. As he walked through Priesty Fields — a beauty spot between Astbury and Congleton in Cheshire — he noticed something floating in Howty Brook. On his instructions, one of the two lads with him, 13-year-old Will Barrett, jumped into the brook which was swollen due to recent heavy rain. The boy grasped what he thought was a woman's blue cloak, but on pulling it to the bank he discovered it was a blue dress, saturated with blood. The water, likewise, was clouded red.

After sending Barrett hurrying off to find a constable, Garside himself waded into the water. Swishing his hands around, he pulled out a petticoat, a blue cloak and an old apron. In the apron's pockets he found a small, half-eaten brown loaf, an old tobacco box, a case of needles and thread, a pair of scissors, a thimble and two ballads.

Reaching further down into the water he felt something hard and round like a rock. He pulled it up. To his horror, it was the severed head of a young woman. At that moment Barrett returned with Constable John Beswick, who he had met on the road.

Examining the head, the policeman wiped away the blood and river-muck and found two knife cuts on each jaw and cheek-bone. Realising that more of the corpse was probably in the water, Beswick and Garside made a further search of the brook and discovered a woman's right arm and leg.

The arm had been cut off very neatly at the elbow and the leg at the knee-joint. Another search revealed the left arm and leg, severed in a similar manner.

By this time other men, hearing of the murder at Howty Brook, had stopped work and come to help in the search. Soon several were groping their way along the bottom of the cold brook and bringing up one grotesque find after another.

To gasps of horror from onlookers who included women and children, first a breast, then the bowels, heart, tongue and thighs of the victim were retrieved and laid on the bank. But as night fell, the hunt for body parts had to be called off and the woman's remains were taken by cart to a nearby stable. There they were assembled and it became clear that only one piece was missing — a large section of a calf.

At first light the following morning the authorities began to make enquiries. The murder was by now the talk of the district and it wasn't long before a shopkeeper named Mary Amson came forward. She said that at noon on Wednesday, November 20th, a young woman of about 23 had come into her shop in Astbury and bought a halfpenny-worth of tobacco and a penny loaf. The shopkeeper described the woman, whom she didn't know, as being poorly dressed and wearing a blue cloak and a small black cap.

The police took the witness to the stable and showed her first the murdered woman's clothing and then her head. Hideously disfigured though the features were from immersion in water, the shopkeeper was in no doubt that this was the woman she had served the previous Wednesday.

It was now common knowledge that two ballads had been found amongst the victim's pathetic belongings, and it was soon rumoured that she was a drifter known as "Annie the ballad singer."

A Congleton woman named Mary Fendale told the police that "Annie the ballad-singer," whose name was Annie Smith, had lodged with her until a fortnight ago. On leaving she had said she would return when Congleton Fayre began on Wednesday, November 20th, "if it pleases God to spare me." But she had not come back, which was most unusual because Annie never missed the Fayre.

Mrs. Fendale was also shown the dead woman's head. With tears pouring down her cheeks, she identified it as that of her friend and former lodger. She said that Annie had had a good voice and would earn what she could by singing at local fairs. Because there were few of these in the winter, however, she had recently been reduced to earning what little she could by rag-picking.

As nobody could recall seeing her after noon on November 20th, it was concluded that she had been murdered that afternoon or evening. It could not have been during the night as the killer would have needed a strong light in order to cut her up so expertly.

The murder had made a deep impression on one local man, Tom Cordwell. The 30-year-old weaver had been at the brook side and had watched as the victim's remains were hauled piece by piece from the water.

Sam Thornley had been standing near him. "Horrible, horrible!" Cordwell had heard him mutter. "Who could have done that to her?" Thorley had glanced at Cordwell as he said this and the weaver had nodded in agreement. Later, on making his way home, Cordwell had seen Thorley chatting to two other men, repeatedly stressing that he knew nothing of the murder.

Cordwell arrived home to be told by his wife that Thorley had been named as a suspect in the murder. The weaver's mind began to race. He knew Thorley was simple-minded and had a quick temper. He also knew Thorley was a butcher reputed to enjoy the most gruesome aspects of his calling. It was doubtless his skill with the knife which had caused him to be named as a suspect, the victim having been so professionally dismembered.

Calling on a neighbour, Tom Elkin, Cordwell told him of his suspicions that Thorley was the killer. Elkin had helped the police in their search of Priesty Fields, now regarded as the probable murder scene. He recalled he had noticed blood on a stile near a path which led directly to Hannah Oakes's cottage at Astbury. Mrs. Oakes had once been Thorley's landlady.

Cordwell went at once to examine the stile and found it heavily bloodstained, just as Elkin had described. He then called on the widowed Mrs. Oakes. She confirmed that Sam Thorley had come to see her on the evening of the murder.

She remembered that night very well because it had been particularly cold and windy and she had been loth to open her door. But the knocker persisted and finally she had relented. On the doorstep stood Sam Thorley wearing his butcher's apron — besmirched, as usual, with blood and gore — in which he carried some raw meat.

He was wet up to his waist, Mrs. Oakes recalled, and when she commented on this he told her he had been walking through Priesty Fields when he slipped and fell into Howty Brook. However, he had landed on his feet and hadn't dropped the meat, which he now thumped down on her kitchen table.

When Mrs. Oakes asked him where he'd got it, he said that a farmer had been driving a pig along Congleton High Street when the animal suddenly collapsed. As a crowd gathered, someone had pointed Sam out to the farmer as a butcher, saying that he would gladly finish the pig off for him. Thorley claimed he had then killed the creature and bled it. As a reward the farmer had given him some of the pork.

Mrs. Oakes examined it. To her experienced eye it didn't look fit to eat. She recalled that Sam had seemed strangely excited, wanting her to boil it there and then so he could eat it. She refused, but had allowed him to leave the meat with her.

The following evening, Thursday, November 21st, Thorley had returned to her cottage and boiled the meat for himself. He then sat down to eat it, but after a few mouthfuls he was violently sick — confirming Mrs. Oakes' suspicions that the meat was "off."

Pushing his plate from him, Thorley had told her that he would eat no more and she could give the rest to her dogs. But Mrs. Oakes thought it unfit even for a dog to eat and told the butcher she would throw it away.

Cordwell's heart sank when he heard this, thinking that the "evidence" had been disposed of, probably on the midden where rats would have gnawed it to nothing.

But Mrs. Oakes was too frugal to throw things away. She went on to say she'd had second thoughts and had decided to boil a little of the meat up for grease. The rest she had kept to use for the same purpose in the future.

Cordwell asked to see it. Taking it out of the oven where

she had stored it, Mrs. Oakes put it on the table. Cordwell was shocked to see that it looked and felt like the dead woman's missing calf.

"God forbid!" screamed Mrs. Oakes. "He told me it was pork!"

Cordwell went at once to the police who called in a surgeon to examine Mrs. Oakes's meat. He confirmed that it was human flesh.

That afternoon Annie Smith's inquest was held at Congleton Town Hall. The jury listened in horror as Mrs. Oakes described the meat Sam Thorley had brought to her cottage on the night of the murder, and his abortive attempts to eat it the next evening.

She went on to say that Thorley had called to see her that very morning at nine o'clock, prior to Tom Cordwell's visit. As they discussed the murder she had reminded Thorley of his visit on the night of the crime and asked if he had heard or seen anything suspicious.

Thorley said he hadn't, and became angry at the implication that he was a suspect. Mrs. Oakes told the jury she had calmed him by saying, "I did not think it was thee, Sam."

Placated, the butcher had sat back in his chair, announcing: "I would not have done it for ten pounds or twenty pounds. Nay, nor for a thousand."

At the conclusion of the evidence the jury returned a verdict of wilful murder against Sam Thorley, and shortly afterwards he was arrested at his lodgings in Astbury's School Lane.

After he had spent 128 days in the foul dungeons of Chester Castle, his trial before Mr. Justice Moreton took place at Chester Assizes on April 3rd, 1777.

Thorley's explanation for the murder was that he had been told human flesh resembled young pig in taste. Having a liking for raw meat he had decided to find out if this were true. In view of this confession his trial was little more than a formality.

He was hanged on April 10th, 1777, at Boughton, just

outside Chester, before spectators who travelled many miles to witness the end of the notorious "Congleton Cannibal."

As the noose was slipped around his neck his sole anxiety seemed to be for his clothes. He was relieved when the executioner assured him he would not take them, as was his right, after the hanging.

Besides being a butcher Sam Thorley was also the grave-digger at Astbury Church, but he was destined never to have a grave of his own. The judge had ordered that after his execution his body would be gibbeted. This meant that his corpse would be disembowelled — sharing the same fate as Annie Smith — and then wrapped in a calico sheet soaked in pitch. A framework of hoop-iron would be riveted around his body and the whole thing suspended from a gibbet near the murder scene to deter anyone similarly inclined.

Thorley was thus displayed at 1 p.m. on April 11th, 1777, at West Heath, the nearest suitable spot to Priesty Fields. He was an hour late, his body having fallen off the cart transporting him from Chester as it trundled through Delamere Forest.

Nevertheless when he finally arrived he was greeted by a circus-like atmosphere and the kind of crowd Annie Smith would have entertained with ballads to earn enough pennies for a meal and a bed for the night.

It was later rumoured that Thorley had hawked some of his "pork" around local pubs, and that many customers had become ill. None, however, owned up to being unwitting cannibals!

6
MAD OR BAD?

The **British Medical Journal** *wanted to know why the child had been condemned to death*

FARMER TOM Palliser and his wife Margaret had no complaints about their new servant. Although she had only been with the Pallisers for two weeks, and although she was only thirteen years old, Margaret Messenger was acquitting herself well as the children's nursemaid.

The children liked her too, which is always the real test of a nursemaid, for the Palliser children were a bit of a handful — little Harry, aged two, and two daughters, Margaret, five, and baby Mary, six months, ensured there was always plenty of work for Margaret.

As Tom Palliser finished his lunch and went to sit in his rocking chair in the kitchen for half an hour's rest before returning to the fields the world seemed to him a place of contentment.

On the hearth-rug in front of him little Harry was playing with his toy soldiers. Outside in the yard Margaret Messenger was chopping wood. Mrs. Palliser and her two little daughters were elsewhere in the farmhouse.

Outside, too, on that warm June day at Palliser's farm near Sprunston, four miles outside Carlisle, bees droned around the honeysuckle flowers, swallows dipped and weaved above the buttercups, and the sun shone in a blue sky. In a few minutes Tom's head began to nod, and, lulled by the rural idyll of England in 1881, he fell asleep.

He woke with a sudden start of foreboding. Something was wrong. Swiftly alert, he gazed around him, realising almost at once that what had woken him was the unexpected silence.

Little Harry was no longer on the hearth-rug, where his toy soldiers lay abandoned. Nor was there any longer the sound of chopping from the yard.

"Margaret!" Farmer Palliser called.

The nursemaid hurried into the kitchen, wiping her hands on her apron. No, she hadn't seen the little boy; she'd been too busy outside with her chores.

"Where is the young rascal, then?" muttered Tom. "Search the house for him."

The alarm was quickly sounded. Mrs. Palliser and the other servants came running to help, but there was no sign of little Harry anywhere.

Had he strayed across the field to a neighbouring farm, Tom wondered, and without stopping to think more he pulled on his boots and set out. He had gone only as far as the yard gate when Margaret Messenger called out, "He's here!"

She was standing by the well, pail in hand, looking down in horror. The farmer saw her throw down the pail, bend into the well, and lift out a bundle. It was Harry. He was dead. He must have fallen in and drowned.

When, a few days later, little Harry Palliser was buried in Sprunston churchyard, the whole village was united in grief. Margaret, the nursemaid who had been with the family for so little time, wept uncontrollably at the funeral, for she had quickly become fond of her little charges.

Everyone agreed that the little boy's death was a most unfortunate accident, although some hinted at carelessness that needed a lot of explaining. Why, they asked, had the nursemaid not seen him toddle outside when she was in the yard chopping wood?

And what made her, in the middle of the frantic search, suddenly go across to the well and look for him in there?

Even these sceptics, though, could not possibly have

imagined what would happen next.

On July 2nd, six days after little Harry's death, Mr. and Mrs. Palliser set out for Carlisle market, leaving their two daughters in the care of Margaret Messenger. At 10 o'clock that morning, while the parents were still away, Tom Haffen, a boy working in a field about 100 yards from the Palliser's farmhouse, heard a child scream.

He leaned on his shovel and looked around. It seemed to him that the scream came from the yard of the house. Moments later he heard little Margaret Palliser shout out, "Margaret!" — meaning, he supposed, the nursemaid, for she immediately called back, "I'm here."

Reassured that whatever had happened was now being taken care of by the nursemaid, Haffen thought no more about it and got on with his work. But half an hour later he heard little Margaret calling to him from a field known locally as Lamb's Close.

Haffen hurried over to where the little girl was standing and found her with Margaret Messenger, the nursemaid, who was hysterical. The farm-boy took the nursemaid's arm and shook her.

"What's wrong with you?" he said roughly.

Margaret Messenger, tears streaming down her face, gaped at him in stark terror. "I fell asleep," she mumbled. "I woke up just in time to see a tall man without whiskers running away with baby Mary in his arms." She sobbed pitifully. "Oh, please, please, look for the baby!" she cried.

Haffen shook his head in disbelief. "No one's been around the farm this morning that I know of," he reasoned. But moved by the nursemaid's wet eyes and her fearful looks, he began to search around the field and beyond that, the orchard and the stream.

As Haffen suspected all along, there was no trace of baby Mary or a man without whiskers. "I don't know what you're thinking of," he said, and set off across the field back to his work.

Another hour went by. Looking up suddenly from his digging, Haffen saw the nursemaid coming from the direction of the well. Baby Mary was in her arms, and just the way she held it left him in no doubt that something terrible had happened.

He called out, "Is she dead?"

"Yes," Margaret Messenger shouted back.

Haffen dropped his shovel and ran to the nearest neighbour, Mrs. Storey, who rushed back with him to the Pallisers' yard. Baby Mary was lying on the ground, and despite all the efforts of Mrs. Storey to revive her, the child was beyond all hope.

Carefully Mrs. Storey examined the little body. She noticed that her face and front were muddy, although its back was quite clean, suggesting it had fallen face-down in soft mud. Mrs. Storey went into the farmhouse and found the nursemaid sitting in a chair, weeping.

"What happened?" the neighbour asked.

Still sobbing, Margaret Messenger said, "I fell asleep and when I woke up a man without whiskers was just carrying off the baby. I searched everywhere for it and so did Tom Haffen. I found it lying face-down in the boggy patch of earth near the well."

"We had better wait for your master and mistress to come back, Margaret," Mrs. Storey said icily.

At 3.30 that afternoon Tom Palliser and his wife returned from Carlisle market. With tears still rolling down her cheeks, Margaret Messenger broke the terrible news to them, repeating the story about the man without whiskers but this time adding the detail that he was wearing a straw hat.

All this, coming so soon after the death of little Harry, was too much for the Pallisers, and they broke down. Mrs. Storey did her best to comfort them, then she took Margaret Messenger aside.

"You had better tell me the truth of what happened, girl," she demanded sternly. "No more lies. I want to know how that baby died."

The nursemaid's new story was punctuated with sobs. There had not really been a man without whiskers, she said; she had made up that part of it. What really happened was that she was sitting on some blocks of wood near the house when she fell asleep.

Waking up suddenly, she realised that little Mary was gone. "I thought she must have wandered off somewhere," the nursemaid said, forgetting for the moment that the six-month-old baby could only crawl a few yards. She jumped up and ran around looking for the child, and after alerting Tom Haffen she found the baby near the well, dead.

Mrs. Storey, who thought this tale was as unlikely as the first one, walked thoughtfully over to the well. She looked around, inspecting the ground, and eventually found the indentation of a baby's body in boggy ground between the well and the nearby stream.

She noticed too that a stone was lying close to the outline of the baby's head. The stone had been brought some distance from a pile of other stones. A line of clog-marks in the soft earth led from the farmhouse to the well.

Mrs. Storey, now very much in charge, called Tom Haffen over from his work in the field. "You had better get off to Carlisle and bring the police," she said. "I think the baby's been murdered."

A few hours later the commendable Mrs. Storey was telling Superintendent Sempill, of Carlisle police, what she had found. The officer took casts of the clog-marks — which turned out to be the same shape and size as Margaret Messenger's.

While he was inspecting the crime scene Mrs. Storey told the weeping Margaret Messenger that it looked very bad for her. "You would do better to tell the truth," she said. "The police will find out the truth, and then these stories of yours will be held against you."

Drying her tears, Margaret Messenger suddenly leapt up. "I'll tell you what happened," she said, as if in great excitement. "I did it myself and no one helped me."

When Superintendent Sempill came back into the farmhouse she confessed again with just as much enthusiasm. She was arrested and taken to Carlisle.

The post-mortem on little Mary revealed mud in her lungs as well as in her mouth, causing her to suffocate. There were several marks on her head which could have been caused by the stone found near the body.

Margaret Messenger spent her 14th birthday on remand in jail and was brought before Mr. Justice Kay at Cumberland Assizes on November 2nd, 1881, charged with the murder of the baby. She now retracted her confession and pleaded not guilty.

Her defence was yet another concocted story. She had left little Mary in charge of her older sister, she said, and the baby must have crawled off, fallen into a puddle by the well and drowned. The older sister was in court to corroborate this version.

The child had died by accident, the nursemaid's counsel insisted, and no one could be held to blame for what had happened.

The judge made it clear in his summing-up that he was far from convinced by this new tale. He told the jury, "If this theory were correct, a stone would not have been found by the child's head, in a place where there were no other stones.

"The only question for you is whether you can arrive at the conclusion that the baby could in any way have come by its death except by the act of the prisoner."

It took 10 minutes for the jury to agree with the judge, adding to their guilty verdict a strong recommendation for mercy on the grounds of the nursemaid's age.

A deathly silence fell on the court then, for in 1881 the law made no distinction between child and adult offenders, and the mandatory sentence for murder was death by hanging. The black cap was set on the judge's head, and clearly distressed, in a faltering, barely audible voice he sentenced Margaret Messenger to death.

A newspaper reporter wrote: "A most painful feeling pervaded the court and many women sobbed aloud."

Where the trial of Margaret Messenger and the

sentencing of her was now patently unjust lay in the fact that the tragic fate of little Harry Palliser while in her care was never mentioned by either defence or prosecution. If it had been raised only in mitigation after the verdict, it would have given the judge an opportunity to consider her state of mind.

It might then have been difficult for anyone to dispute the proposition that a child who commits two murders without motive must be at least temporarily insane.

The sentence had the whole country agog — everyone was asking, would the system really allow a 14-year-old girl to hang? The answer came swiftly. The Home Secretary, Sir William Harcourt, decided that it could not happen, and Margaret Messenger was reprieved almost as soon as she was sentenced.

But that wasn't the end of the matter — for the next question was, what was going to happen to the teenage killer? The influential *British Medical Journal* was particularly critical of the court proceedings.

It asked, why the child had been condemned to death in the first place "by a deeply affected judge and a courtroom in tears. Are such scenes likely to promote good morale or to deter the commission of crime?"

The journal raised doubts as to Margaret's fitness to stand trial from the outset. "No motive is suggested for the crime to which the girl confessed, after having made one or two contradictory statements about the death of the baby.

"It was reported in the district, though not mentioned at the trial, that an infant previously entrusted to the girl's care died under very suspicious circumstances.

"Should this rumour prove to be well founded there would be additional grounds for believing that the wretched girl labours under a form of insanity with homicidal impulses, that has been observed to develop itself occasionally at puberty."

The journal suggested that Margaret should be thoroughly examined and her state of mind established. If she were a lunatic she should not be made to undergo penal servitude for life, which was then, for children and adults alike, the mandatory sentence for prisoners reprieved from a capital sentence.

It declared: "Medical jurisprudence will not be satisfied nor the public conscience quieted, until it is determined whether this unhappy girl is a murderess or a lunatic."

The journal's comments were widely reported and as a result Dr. William Orange, medical superintendent at Broadmoor, examined Margaret on November 10th, 1881. Whether she should go into his care or to prison would depend upon his assessment.

During the examination at Carlisle Prison she told Dr. Orange that she murdered little Harry Palliser. She could give no reason why. The idea had simply occurred to her, she said, while she was chopping wood in the yard.

She put down the axe she was using, took the little boy by the hand, led him to the well and threw him in.

Dr. Orange's conclusions were unfortunately not made public, so no one knows whether he thought Margaret was mad or just bad. But on December 14th the Home Secretary announced that she would serve penal servitude for life. Whether that meant that Dr. Orange was not convinced she was mad, or that his recommendations were ignored, remains a mystery.

The reprieve meant that the 14-year-old girl would spend at least 20 years in a convict prison — she would probably have been released at some time in her mid-thirties. Nothing more was ever heard of her again.

7
THE BLACKPOOL POISONER

"He's a very greedy old bugger"

"A QUARRELSOME and difficult old woman," —
that was how many people in Blackpool saw Mrs.
Sarah Ann Ricketts. The twice-widowed 79-year-old had
fallen out with nearly all her friends and most of her
family, including her two daughters — one of whom she
accused of stealing blankets and curtains from her home,
while the other she described as "one of the biggest
prostitutes in Blackpool." Not surprisingly, neither of the
daughters visited her very often.

But Mrs. Ricketts needed to be looked after. Although
in general good health and young-looking for her age, she
had a paralysed arm which made it impossible for her to
care for herself properly, so she advertised for a housekeeper. On March 11th, 1953, 46-year-old Mrs. Louisa
Merrifield and her 71-year-old husband Alfred applied for
the position and were immediately accepted. Instead of a
salary, Mrs. Ricketts offered them free accommodation in
her smart modern detached bungalow, The Homestead, in
Devonshire Road, although they would have to pay their
own heating, lighting and food bills. This seemed an
acceptable arrangement and the Merrifields moved in the
next day.

Incredibly, in just seven days the dumpy, bespectacled
Mrs. Merrifield and her elderly, partially deaf husband
proved themselves so indispensable to Mrs. Ricketts that

she told them: "If you do justice to me and look after me, I will see you have a home for life. I will send for a solicitor and have a will drawn up in your favour." And on March 31st she summoned her solicitor and dictated a new will, leaving her bungalow — worth between £3,000 and £4,000 — jointly to the Merrifields, together with other personal property.

Having spent the last two years drifting from one menial live-in job to the next, the couple could hardly believe their good fortune. They didn't know that this was the sixth will Mrs. Ricketts had made in the last 10 years and that she had more than once bequeathed the bungalow to others in her employ, only to change her mind shortly afterwards.

The ink had hardly dried on the document before, true to form, she began having second thoughts. In the days that followed she complained to anyone who called at the bungalow that the Merrifields were going through her money very quickly and were not giving her enough to eat. Finally, on the morning of April 13th, in the hearing of a delivery man she told them they would have to go. Turning to Mr. Merrifield, she went on: "When you go to the bank will you also go to my solicitors because I want to change my will." But Mr. Merrifield told her it was too far for him to walk to the solicitors as well as to the bank.

At 1.50 the following afternoon Dr. Burton Yule arrived at the bungalow to find Mrs. Ricketts dead in bed. He was immediately suspicious, as he had examined her only four days earlier when she had been in perfect health. Finding nothing to account for her sudden demise, he refused to sign a death certificate and notified the coroner's office. That night a post-mortem was carried out and yellow phosphorus was found in Mrs. Ricketts's stomach. The police were informed and Detective Superintendent Colin McDougall arrived from Scotland Yard.

As yellow phosphorus was in rat poison, he had the bungalow searched. When his men drew a blank they took a metal-detector and examined the garden, but again found nothing. As they swarmed around the bungalow which had a history of sudden death — both Mrs. Ricketts's husbands had committed suicide there — a Salvation Army band appeared at the gate and began playing *Abide With Me*. They had been summoned by Mrs. Merrifield, a Salvationist, as a mark of respect for her deceased employer.

Without the poison the police had little evidence against the Merrifields, but Mrs. Merrifield's behaviour was highly suspicious. The moment the old lady was dead she had called an undertaker and asked him to arrange cremation "at once," but without a death certificate this was impossible.

Mrs. Merrifield had also taken a large handbag from the bungalow which she asked a friend to keep for her. This was eventually given to the police, who found a dessertspoon coated with a gritty residue which an analyst believed could have formed if the spoon had been used to mix phosphorus with rum. But there was no trace of phosphorus, which evaporates when exposed to the air.

Local residents came forward when it became known that the Merrifields were suspects. They informed the police that Mrs. Merrifield had told them that Mrs. Ricketts had died, leaving the couple her bungalow, days, sometimes weeks, before her actual death!

On March 19th, just one week after she began working for Mrs. Ricketts, Mrs. Merrifield had bumped into an acquaintance, Mrs. Harriet Allwood. She told her excitedly that she was now living with a very nice old lady, adding: "It looks to me as if she thinks a lot of me and she will probably leave me the house."

Mrs. Allwood was astonished. "But you've not been there five minutes yet!" she said. On March 25th, six days before the will was drawn up and three weeks before Mrs. Ricketts died, Mrs. Merrifield met a former workmate, David Brindley, and told him: "Oh, David, I have had a bit of good luck where I have been living. The old lady has died and left me a bungalow worth about three thousand pounds."

On March 30th, the day before the will was signed, Mrs. Merrifield had written to her friend Mrs. Lowe: "I've got a nice job nursing an old lady and she has left me a lovely little bungalow. Thank God for it." On April 11th, four days before Mrs. Ricketts died, Mrs. Merrifield had told a former employer, Mrs. Jessie Brewer: "We are landed. We went to live with an old lady and she died and she has left me a bungalow worth four thousand pounds." But Mrs. Merrifield seemed annoyed that her husband had been included in the will, telling Mrs. Brewer that Mrs. Ricketts would have left everything to her alone, "if that old bugger [Mr. Merrifield] had not talked to her."

The next day, April 12th, Mrs. Merrifield had visited her friend Mrs. Veronica King, telling her: "I will have to be going now. I have got to lay an old lady out." Surprised, Mrs. King asked if Mrs. Ricketts was dead. "No, but she soon will be," Mrs. Merrifield had replied with a grin.

The next morning, while waiting for a bus, Mrs. Merrifield struck up a conversation with a complete stranger, Mrs. Elizabeth Barraclough, telling her: "I am very worried. I am looking after an old lady who is very ill. She is leaving a bungalow between me and my husband. But he's a very greedy old bugger. He wants her to leave the bungalow to him. I was away yesterday at Wigan visiting my two children [this was a lie — she had been visiting Mrs. King] and when I got back my husband was in bed with the old lady. If this goes on again I will poison the old so-and-so and him as well."

The following afternoon Mrs. Ricketts was pronounced dead.

The handbag containing the dessertspoon also held numerous documents relating to Mrs. Merrifield's life. These included insurance policies — two had been taken out on the life of her husband Alfred. Detectives suspected that Mrs. Merrifield had taken the handbag from the bungalow before they searched it because she felt the details of her past life would not bear close scrutiny.

They were right. Investigating her background, they

learned that she was born Louisa May Heighway in Cowburn Street, Hindley, Wigan, on December 1st, 1906, the youngest child of a miner. After leaving school at 13 she had taken a variety of domestic jobs before becoming a cook. In 1931 she had married Joe Ellison, an ironworker, bearing him seven children of whom only four survived.

As her husband suffered from tuberculosis and was unable to work, she took in lodgers. But she preferred drinking in the local pubs to looking after her sick husband and children, and in 1947 complaints from her neighbours resulted in her three younger children being taken into care. She later applied to get them back, but her application was rejected because of her reputation.

Although she always insisted on her lodgers paying their rent on time, she rarely paid her own bills. During the war she had been convicted of stealing two ration books from a neighbour and was fined £20. Refusing to pay, she had spent two months in Manchester's Strangeways Prison.

Many in Wigan remembered her as a persuasive talker. A shopkeeper recalled: "She could tell a tale which would bring the ducks off the water. She told such plausible tales that I found myself acting against my better judgement and letting her have what she wanted."

Joe Ellison died in October 1949, and two months later she married one of her lodgers, 78-year-old Richard Weston, a retired colliery under-manager who died of a heart attack two months after their wedding. Four months later she married another of her lodgers, widower Alfred Edward Merrifield, a retired sanitary-ware maker and the father of 10 children.

The couple had moved to Blackpool in April 1951, Louisa working as a cook and general domestic and occasionally nursing people. In the two years prior to meeting Mrs. Ricketts, the couple had between them held 20 such jobs in the resort.

Understandably, they had found it very difficult to live on Mr. Merrifield's weekly pension of 32s. 6d. (£1. 62½), a little National Assistance and their earnings from menial work. So the promise of a £4,000 bungalow would have been a strong motive for murder, the police decided, and the Merrifields were arrested.

It had been established that they could have obtained yellow phosphorus through buying rat poison. Rodine, a well-known brand usually sold in one or two shilling tins, contained about ten grains of yellow phosphorus — enough to kill at least five people. The only other ingredient of Rodine was bran, and this had been found in Mrs. Ricketts's stomach.

Shortly after her arrest Mrs. Merrifield told the police that Mrs. Ricketts had nothing to eat the evening before her death which could account for the presence of bran.

Mrs. Lavinia Blezzard, a home-help employed by Mrs. Ricketts prior to the appointment of the Merrifields', told detectives that the widow never kept rat poison in the house, but there was strong evidence that Alfred Merrifield had bought a tin of Rodine from a chemist in Victoria Bridge, Manchester, in late March, 1953. At an identification parade both the chemist and his assistant picked him out as a man to whom they had sold a tin of Rodine at about that time.

Louisa Merrifield looked relaxed and composed in her grey hat and coat when the couple, charged with Mrs. Ricketts's murder, appeared at Manchester Assizes on July 20th, 1953. In the witness box she insisted that she had loved the old lady and would never have harmed her. She also denied telling friends she had inherited the bungalow when in fact Mrs. Ricketts was still alive. These witnesses, she said, had told lies about her "out of envy as they are up to their necks in mortgages."

Describing Mrs. Ricketts as "whimsical and strong-willed," Mrs. Merrifield maintained that the elderly widow had been a very sick woman. Besides being paralysed in one arm, she had a drink problem and Mrs. Merrifield said that despite her best efforts, her employer often preferred alcohol to food. But Mrs. Ricketts's usual diet of egg and brandy three times a day began to cause problems. "I told her that she could not have the nourishing foods, spirits, and other things on her income," said Mrs. Merrifield. "They were too expensive."

The prosecution later pointed out that Mrs. Ricketts had a weekly income of £6, which was more than sufficient for all her needs. But in the witness box Mrs. Merrifield continued: "She told me that she had managed before I came, but I told her that she was now having more food and it was better than drink. But Mrs. Ricketts took her own money and carried on buying drink and neglecting food. On Thursday, April 9th, I saw a change in her when she did not get the food. I asked her who was her doctor and she said she had not had one for two years.

"After she complained of stomach pains I asked her again who her doctor was and suggested Dr. Wood, who lived close by. But she said she would not have him or his men. Later that day I went to see Dr. Yule and asked him to visit Mrs. Ricketts."

Mrs. Merrifield had also paid the doctor 10s. 6d. to certify that the old lady was capable of signing the new will she had recently made in the couple's favour. This was doubtless a precaution in case Mrs. Ricketts's daughters later challenged the will.

"Dr. Yule came the next day," Mrs. Merrifield recalled, "and asked Mrs. Ricketts if she had made her will. She replied, 'I'm looking after them that are looking after me.' The doctor said: 'You are quite *compos mentis* and know what you are doing?' 'Definitely,' was the old lady's reply. Mrs. Ricketts was very ill on Sunday, April 12th, but managed to consume five eggs, brandy, liquid paraffin, rum, stout and use two pounds of blackcurrant jam in drinking, mixing spirits with it.

"Next day she was still unwell and I went for Dr. Wood. I stayed up with her till midnight and heard her moaning. She was rubbing her stomach. She was out of bed and I got her in again. At 1 a.m. I gave her an egg-cupful of rum. I then returned to bed. At 3.15 a.m. I heard her moving about again, and getting up I found her sitting on the hall floor. I picked her up and brought her to bed. She said she was thankful to me and my husband for all we had done for her. These were the last words she spoke. I kept giving her brandy. She just kept putting her tongue out and opening her mouth for a drink.''

Mrs. Merrifield went on to say that when there was no improvement in Mrs. Ricketts's condition by 8.20 a.m., she again went for Dr. Wood. As he was not available his partner Dr. Page called at the house at lunch-time. Mrs. Ricketts looked at him but was unable to speak. The doctor said he could not examine her as she was not his patient and suggested to the housekeeper that she see Dr. Yule.

Mrs. Merrifield claimed that she called on Mrs. Yule three times before she said she would send her husband. On returning home after doing some shopping she found Dr. Yule examining Mrs. Ricketts, who was by this time dead.

Cross-examining Mrs. Merrifield, the Attorney General, Sir Lionel Heald QC, prosecuting, asked her why she hadn't called a doctor at 3.15 a.m.

''Well, it was not such a nice time in the morning to go out in the streets and call a doctor,'' she replied.

''Isn't there another explanation?'' asked Sir Lionel. ''That is, you saw the old lady was going and wanted her to go?''

Dr. Yule testified that when Mrs. Merrifield called at his surgery on April 9th to ask him to certify that Mrs. Ricketts was mentally competent, she said nothing about Mrs. Ricketts being ill. When he called the next day Mrs. Ricketts didn't want to be examined, but when she relented he concluded that she was in very good health for her age and her wits, like her tongue, were as sharp as ever. She made no complaint about feeling unwell, and he was therefore suspicious when four days later, knowing that the Merrifields stood to inherit Mrs. Ricketts's estate, he was summoned to the house to find her dead in bed from no apparent cause.

Dr. Wood had died since being summoned by Mrs. Merrifield to examine Mrs. Ricketts during the evening prior to her death, but he had made out a deposition which was now read out in court. He recalled that he had been feeling ill and had not wanted to attend Mrs. Ricketts, but Mrs. Merrifield had led him to believe that the patient might be dying. So when he found Mrs. Ricketts to be perfectly well he felt that he had been called out on false pretences.

Dr. Ernest Page then gave evidence about the events of the following morning, April 14th. He said he arrived at the bungalow at about 12 noon to find Mr. Merrifield having his lunch in Mrs. Ricketts's bedroom. He was sitting so close to the patient's bed that the doctor had to push him aside in order to reach her. She was unable to speak, and as she wasn't his patient Dr. Page had advised Mrs. Merrifield to send for Dr. Yule, adding that he thought Mrs. Ricketts was dying. The housekeeper had shrugged, saying; "She's over eighty and has been dying since we came to the place."

Mr. Merrifield now went into the witness box. He had already broken down once during the trial, moaning, "I can't stick any more," and weeping as his wife beside him in the dock patted him consolingly on the shoulder. His discomfort was intensified by the fact that his hearing-aid was malfunctioning and he often couldn't hear what was being said.

When the prosecutor suddenly produced a tin of Rodine from behind his back, the old man covered his face and turned away crying, "Don't let me look at it! I have heard so much about it this last four months, I see it in my sleep!"

"You have seen something like this before?" demanded Sir Lionel.

Visibly trembling, Merrifield replied: "No, unless it has been in some shop or chemist's shop when I have had occasion to enter."

"You have seen it?" Sir Lionel persisted.

"I have not seen it," Merrifield repeated, "and don't ask me again. Definitely I have not seen it." Then he burst into tears.

The prosecution claimed that the Merrifields' murder motive was inheriting the bungalow, coupled with the fact that Mrs. Ricketts had been about to change her will, leaving them nothing. And they had the opportunity — they were alone with Mrs. Ricketts when she died and had prepared all her food and drink. Although Mrs. Merrifield had told the court she had tried to do her best for the old lady, many witnesses had testified that she had in fact spent most of her time drinking in local pubs.

Although Professor J. M. Webster, director of Birmingham's forensic laboratory, said he thought that Mrs. Ricketts had died from liver necrosis due to heavy drinking with insufficient food, the Home Office pathologist Dr. G. B. Manning testified that he had found nothing in her liver that might have resulted from excessive alcohol. Dr. Yule had also stated that he had not noticed any sign of alcohol abuse, and Mrs. Ricketts's former cleaning lady, Mrs. Blezzard, said she had never seen her drunk, although the widow had rum in her tea morning and evening, and a small bottle of stout for "elevenses."

For the defence Mr. Jack de V. Nahum QC argued that Rodine was so foul-tasting and smelling that Mrs. Ricketts would have refused to drink it. But tests made by Dr. Manning had found that if it were mixed with rum — Mrs. Ricketts's favourite tipple — both the taste and smell were masked. And Mrs. Merrifield had testified that she had given Mrs. Ricketts an egg-cupful of rum in the hours preceding her death.

During his summing-up Mr. Justice Glyn-Jones described Mrs. Merrifield as "a vulgar and stupid woman." He also said she had a dirty mind. She had claimed that while she was bathing Mrs. Ricketts the old lady had asked her to perform an "immoral act." Mrs. Merrifield had said she was at first shocked, but then thought that having been a widow for 10 years Mrs. Ricketts was probably feeling sexually deprived. However, her sympathy for Mrs. Ricketts had quickly evaporated when she returned home one day and found her in bed with her husband.

Alfred Merrifield had denied having sex with Mrs. Ricketts, claiming that the only intimacy that took place between them was during the occasional times he had massaged her legs to relieve her arthritis. Pointing to his wife he had added: "What could I want with an old lady when I have a young woman to satisfy my needs?"

But Mrs. Merrifield had claimed that his interest in the old lady wasn't entirely sexual. She said he had hoped she would change her mind and leave the bungalow to him alone.

At the conclusion of the 11-day trial the jury deliberated for nearly six hours. Then they found Mrs. Merrifield guilty of murder, but were unable to reach a verdict on her husband, whom the defence had described as a "tragic simpleton." Louisa Merrifield was sentenced to death for what the judge described as "a secret and treacherous crime," and Alfred Merrifield was discharged.

Infuriated by newspaper reports of her husband's remarks about her, Mrs. Merrifield refused five times to see him when he tried to visit her at Strangeways Prison.

In an interview Merrifield had said of his wife: "I have learned from bitter experience that she has no feelings for the old man she married. In the short time while we were together she dragged my good name in the mud. She ill-treated me so badly and so often that my health broke down. She showed no pity, not even ordinary womanly kindness. Not for all the money in the world would I live in the same house as Louise again. I would prefer a thousand miles between us."

However, on the evening of September 16th, two days before her execution and shortly after she learned she was not to be reprieved, Mrs. Merrifield finally agreed to see her husband. They talked for 45 minutes and when he left her she was in tears. Her last words to him were: "Goodbye, Alfie, look after yourself. God bless you."

At 9 a.m. on Friday, September 18th, 1953, Mrs. Louisa May Merrifield became the first woman to be hanged in Britain since the execution of 42-year-old Margaret Allen, the Rawtenstall murderess, at Strangeways on January 12th, 1949. Albert Pierrepoint was the hangman, and 400 people kept vigil in pouring rain outside the prison while at nearby Manchester Cathedral, Alfred Merrifield prayed for his wife's soul.

He subsequently received his half-share in the bungalow and spent the rest of his life making lucrative appearances in Blackpool sideshows as the "Husband of the Blackpool Poisoner," dying in 1962, aged 80.

A newspaper reporter who covered the trial later commented: "It was her wagging tongue that provided the evidence that damned Mrs. Merrifield as a liar and convicted her. She had always wanted to appear 'one better' than her friends and neighbours. She spent her life in the pursuit of money and security to the exclusion of all else — even her own children — and was prepared even to murder to get what she wanted."

8
THE MURDER OF ALBERT DEWHURST

If only the tram had been late that morning

ON EASTER Monday, 1906, Albert Dewhurst, 42, closed his butcher's shop in Church Street, Preston, and took his wife Margaret, 38, and their 10-year-old daughter Mary to Blackpool for the day. It was so warm and sunny it could have been July and the Dewhursts, like the other families who had flocked to the Lancashire resort, were determined to make the most of the good weather.

Mr. Dewhurst hoped the trip might improve his wife's health. The couple had been married 11 years and had three children, but only Mary had survived infancy. Mrs. Dewhurst, both physically and mentally, had never fully recovered from the trauma of those losses.

Although she was an excellent mother to Mary and an efficient worker in her husband's shop, the strain was beginning to tell. She was always tired and had recently been complaining of pains in her head. These were sometimes so severe that she would have to go to bed until they eased.

Knowing she was fed-up with the butchering business, Albert had promised to retire soon and concentrate instead on the buying and selling of livestock. Although pleased by this, Margaret continued to be depressed and withdrawn.

Nevertheless, the Dewhursts remained, outwardly at least, a content couple. As they strolled along the promenade arm in arm, little Mary running happily in front of them, nobody would have suspected what was to come.

At 6.30 on the morning of Wednesday, April 18th — two days after the trip to Blackpool — Mr. Dewhurst was preparing to open his shop. When Sam Massey the assistant arrived, he found his boss already hard at work cutting up meat for the window.

As they exchanged good-mornings Mrs. Dewhurst came hurrying down the stairs, straightening her hair and looking upset. Sam, knowing she suffered ill-health, supposed she was just feeling off-colour. Mr. Dewhurst, glancing at his pocket-watch, announced that he was going to the cattle market — it was time for his usual weekly visit. He looked across at his wife.

"You'll be able to manage now? I'm going to get ready for the market."

"All right, I can manage," she replied.

Taking off his apron, the butcher put on his coat and hat and set off to catch the 7.15 a.m. tram. However, he hadn't been gone more than a few minutes when he returned disappointed, saying that the tram had gone. He'd missed it.

"Catch a later one," advised Sam.

"I'll have to," said Dewhurst as he made his way to the kitchen at the rear of the shop. Mrs. Dewhurst, who was cutting up meat, said nothing. But when her husband returned from the kitchen a few moments later, intending to catch the next tram, she met him at the door.

Neither spoke. Then Sam, hearing Dewhurst cry out as if in great pain, swung round to see him clutching his stomach, from which blood was gushing. To his horror he saw Mrs. Dewhurst standing over her husband holding two bloodstained knives, and with a strange, mad look on her face. In a desperate attempt to escape her Dewhurst staggered towards the front door, calling out for help, but he fell before he could reach it.

Mrs. Dewhurst disappeared into the kitchen. Sam dashed after her and found her standing there waving a knife around and "looking very wild and excited." He seized her arm and the knife dropped to the floor. But he failed to hold her and she struggled free, so he ran back into the shop to see what he could do for her husband.

As Sam was struggling with Mrs. Dewhurst in the kitchen, PC Jones, on duty in Church Street, noticed a crowd gathering at the window of Dewhurst's shop, and went to investigate. When he peered through the glass-panelled door and saw a man lying on the floor covered in blood, he forced his way in. Mr. Dewhurst was still alive, but so weak through loss of blood that he couldn't answer when the policeman asked him: "Who has done this?"

After sending someone in the crowd to fetch Dr. Rayner, who lived nearby, Jones did what he could to staunch the blood flowing from the butcher's wounds. By then Sam Massey had arrived at Dewhurst's side and told the constable what had happened.

Looking around for Mrs. Dewhurst, the policeman spotted her by the stairs, but when he approached her she bolted up them, a knife in each hand. Following her, he found she had barricaded herself in a back bedroom. He put his shoulder to the door and managed to burst it open at the first attempt. An appalling sight met his eyes. Mrs. Dewhurst, the two knives held aloft, was standing over her daughter, who cowered in fear beneath her bedclothes.

"Oh, don't Mamma, don't!" Mary pleaded as her mother struck wildly at her.

Jones dived at the woman and tried to pinion her arms, but though he was young and strong he couldn't subdue her. At that moment PC Winder arrived, and with his help Mrs. Dewhurst was finally overpowered and taken down-stairs.

Meanwhile Dr. Rayner had arrived. Finding that Mr. Dewhurst was too weak to be taken to hospital, he had him carried into the kitchen and laid on a sofa.

There was little the doctor could do, and the butcher died a few minutes later.

On her arrival at the police station Mrs. Dewhurst sat quietly on the seat offered her while PC Jones made out his report. She appeared to have no recollection of what had just happened, and on being charged with her husband's murder she replied in surprise: "He's not dead, is he?"

Brought before the magistrates at Preston's Sessions House that afternoon, she looked demented, with wild, staring eyes and her hair dishevelled. On the third finger of her left hand — her ring finger – she wore a bandage, having cut herself during her struggle with the two policemen. She appeared to be oblivious to the proceedings and to the crowd which had packed the courtroom.

Dr. Rayner, who had performed a post-mortem examination, testified that Albert Dewhurst had died from a haemorrhage caused by two stab wounds, one to the chest and the other to the abdomen. It was the latter which had proved fatal. The butcher's knives wrested from Mrs. Dewhurst by the constables had been the murder weapons.

Sam Massey told the court he had worked for Mr. Dewhurst for three years and had never heard a cross word between the butcher and his wife. Other witnesses also testified that the couple appeared to have a happy relationship.

Then, as PC Jones was giving his evidence, Margaret Dewhurst collapsed in a fit and had to be carried from the court, foaming at the mouth and struggling. Despite this she was committed for trial at the next Liverpool Assizes, charged with her husband's murder.

The "Preston Tragedy," as the murder had quickly become known, had caused a sensation in the town, and people came from far and wide to see the shop in Church Street and to peer through the shuttered windows.

In the hope of some privacy, the funeral of Albert Dewhurst was arranged for 9.30 a.m. on Saturday, April 21st. Yet despite the early hour, huge crowds gathered around the shop to see the cortège set off, while equally large numbers lined the route to Preston Cemetery.

But there was one notable absentee from the graveside. Margaret Dewhurst was now lying seriously ill in Preston Prison Infirmary, tended around the clock by four nurses. She had no memory of her husband's death and frequently asked for him. She also asked for her daughter, but failed to recognise anyone who went to see her. The doctor caring for her believed that the pains in the head of which she had so often complained could have brought on a fit of temporary insanity, during which she stabbed her husband.

On May 7th, 1906, Margaret Alice Dewhurst, in better physical if not mental health, appeared at Liverpool Assizes before Mr. Justice Bigham. Dressed in deepest black, she sat in the dock with her eyes downcast and an expression of total dejection.

Dr. Price, Chief Medical Officer at Liverpool's Walton Prison, told the court that since Mrs. Dewhurst had been in his care she had always been in a state of deep depression, and he had been able only to get monosyllabic answers to his questions. He considered her mental stupor would make it impossible for her to follow the trial proceedings, and she would therefore be unfit to plead. He added that there was a history of insanity in her family and that one sister was confined in an asylum.

The judge then ordered Mrs. Dewhurst to be detained during His Majesty's Pleasure, and she was removed from the dock apparently unaware of what had been said. Her destination was Broadmoor criminal lunatic asylum, where the release of a killer, even one who was "cured," was virtually unknown and most patients could be expected to spend the rest of their days at the hospital.

Mary Dewhurst, who had been so close to death at her mother's hands, was placed in the seclusion of a local Roman Catholic convent where it was hoped she would eventually recover from her ordeal. She must often have wondered how things would have turned out had her father not missed the tram that fatal morning ...

9

THE OLDHAM WAKES WEEK MURDER

"Dear Sir, Miss Sunderland knows as much as me about the Hollins Road crime"

FRANK RATCLIFFE was puzzled. He earned his living as a "knocker-up," his badge of office being the long pole he carried to wake his Oldham millworker customers by rattling their front bedroom windows — few working folk could afford an alarm clock in the 1890s. And what puzzled him was the mystery of 412 Hollins Road.

No matter how early in the morning he passed Joe Mellor's home, there was always a light burning. Nobody left a lamp burning all night unless there was illness in the house, but Joe Mellor's wife was said to be away at her mother's. And it was common knowledge that Joe no longer slept at home but at the mill where he worked as a storeman and to which he had a key. So why did he leave a light burning all night in an empty house? The knocker-up couldn't make it out.

Joe Mellor, 33, and his wife Mary Jane, 36, had lived in Hollins Road for five years. For the first two years they had simply lived together "over the brush," as it was called. Then on August 31st, 1889, they had married at St. George's Church, Hyde, where Mary Jane — or Jenny, as she was known — had originally come from.

To their neighbours they seemed reasonably happy, if not particularly well suited. While Joe was a quiet, temperate, hard-working man, Jenny was sluttish, with a liking for drink and a tendency to use bad language.

To the couple's sorrow, they were childless. To compensate for this, Jenny would often take out the daughter of a neighbour, Mrs. Emma Chadwick. On the morning of Saturday, September 3rd, 1892, she called as usual at Mrs. Chadwick's terraced house, a few doors from her own, to take the little girl for a walk.

She returned with the child at about two o'clock that afternoon, and for several minutes stood chatting to Mrs. Chadwick, mentioning that she was thinking of visiting her mother in Hyde, "if the weather holds up." The two women then parted, Jenny returning to her own house. And that was the last that was seen of her.

It was the end of Oldham's traditional wakes holiday week, with everyone busily preparing to resume work while their children returned to school, so it was some time before the residents of Hollins Road began to wonder where Jenny Mellor was.

"Gone to see her Mam, who's paralysed," Joe told them. "But I'm expecting her back any day."

Emma Chadwick was suspicious. She remembered her friend telling her she might be visiting her mother, but Jenny had said nothing about her being ill, and Mrs. Chadwick was sure Jenny would have mentioned something as important as that.

Speculation about Jenny's whereabouts was fuelled by the knocker-up's talk of the light left burning all night in Joe Mellor's empty house.

It was noted that Joe's recent behaviour had been strange. Why did he lock the house so securely whenever he left it, and keep all callers at the front door?

In Lancashire nobody locked their front doors in those days ... unless they had something to hide.

As September became October, curiosity about Mrs. Mellor's whereabouts turned to concern. Had her husband done away with her? Or had she run off with another man?

On the morning of October 19th Mrs. Mary Walker, the wife of Mellor's landlord, decided to investigate. Her chance to do so arose because Mellor had failed to bolt the yard door after the sanitary men had visited the house the evening before. Going into the yard, Mrs. Walker tried to peer through the kitchen window, but she could see nothing because a blind had been pulled down.

Undeterred, she fetched a chair and heaving herself up onto it, she was just able to see over the blind and into the kitchen. What she saw astonished her. Flag-stones which formed the floor of the kitchen had been taken up and a large grave-like hole, later to be measured as 6ft 8in long, 3ft wide and 2ft 6in deep, had been dug.

Mrs. Walker fetched her husband, who hurriedly summoned Police Constable Aubrook. The two men then entered the kitchen through the window. It was in a turmoil, with earth piled everywhere and bloodstained clothing lying ripped up in the fireplace.

Aubrook looked through the house, then he decided to search the cellar. He recalled later how he gingerly approached a large carpet stashed in one corner. Pulling back one of the corners, he uncovered the head of Jenny Mellor, joined by sinews alone to the neck of her body lying on its back. When the body was completely uncovered the smell of decomposing flesh was appalling.

Aubrook staggered up the stairs and sent Mr. Walker to fetch a doctor and alert other police officers.

The body was taken away and examined by Dr. Fort, who reported that besides a severe wound on the back of the head Jenny had seven stab-wounds in the left chest wall, two of which had penetrated her heart. Her throat had been so savagely cut that her head was almost severed from her body.

A butcher's knife found in the house and a flat-iron later retrieved from a pawn-broker's, where Mellor had pledged it for 1s 0½d, were identified as the murder weapons.

Police Constable Aubrook went immediately to the mill where Mellor worked. The storeman looked calm when the constable confronted him. "I suppose you know what I've come for?"

Mellor nodded, "Ay, it's all right." But he denied the murdered woman was his wife. "Her name's Stafford, not Mellor," he insisted. It seemed that years earlier Jenny had lived with a man called Stafford in Liverpool, but there was no record that they were ever married.

At first Mellor seemed resigned to his fate, for as he was leaving the mill with Aubrook the policeman heard him say to the cashier, "Pay me up, Robert. I shan't be coming back here any more." But at the police station he denied murdering his wife, claiming that she had accidentally fallen downstairs during an argument. Finding she was dead, he said, he had panicked and decided to bury her in the kitchen. To avoid his neighbours he had returned to the house late in the evenings in order to dig the grave, working all through the night — hence the light seen by the knocker-up. But the post-mortem would prove that the wound on the back of Mrs. Mellor's head was not consistent with a fall, and it was not this injury which had killed her. The knife wounds through her heart had caused her death, and for these Joe had no explanation.

But if there was little doubt that Joe Mellor had murdered his wife, there was much speculation about his motive. Many thought he had killed Jenny for the insurance money. But at the subsequent inquest held at Oldham Town Hall the insurance agent testified that Mrs. Mellor's policy had lapsed weeks before due to non-payment.

The packed courtroom — people had squeezed feet-first through the windows in order to get a seat — then heard from pretty Miss Lizzie Sunderland, 23. Sobbing violently, she admitted she and Mellor had been lovers. She told the astonished court she had known Mellor for five years, ever since he had come to work at the mill where she was employed as a reeler.

Eighteen months ago they had started walking out together, and about a year before the murder Mellor had proposed marriage and she had accepted him. She admitted she had heard rumours that he was married, but he had consistently denied them and she had believed him.

Just before the wakes week holiday he had given her an engagement ring and a date had been set for their wedding in December.

On September 3rd she had been due to meet him at a friend's house in Halifax, where they intended to spend the night together. She had expected him at six o'clock, but he had not arrived until eight. He said he hadn't been able to find the house. Having spent the night together they had returned to Oldham the following day, a Sunday.

To her surprise, Mellor seemed reluctant to go home. Instead he accompanied Lizzie to her parents' house, Nest Farm, Chadderton, where he stayed until 10 o'clock.

Lizzie added, still sobbing, that he had never stayed so late at the house before the wakes. The reason was obvious. Mellor had been late for his appointment on September 3rd, because that day he had murdered his wife, and he had not wanted to return home the following day because all that awaited him there was her putrifying body.

Piqued by the readiness his "fiancée" showed in testifying against him, on the final day of his trial at Manchester Assizes in November 1892, Mellor produced a letter in which he claimed that Lizzie knew as much as he did about the murder.

"Dear Sir, Miss Sunderland knows as much as me about the Hollins Road crime. She has been there four times after 11 o'clock at night since the wakes. I will tell you more after my trial when I will tell all."

A neighbour had seen a woman going into the house late at night, but she was certain it was neither Mrs. Mellor nor Miss Sunderland. Lizzie denied she had ever been to Mellor's house, or that she knew anything about the murder, and the court believed her.

It took the jury 10 minutes to find Mellor guilty of the

wilful murder of his wife, Mary Jane. He showed no emotion, but when the black cap was placed on the judge's head he shouted: "The evidence is false!" To friends in court he called "Goodbye, lads!" as he left the dock.

He was hanged at Strangeways Prison on Tuesday, December 20th, 1892 ... the day he had planned to marry Lizzie.

10
THE DEADLY AMBITION OF ELIZABETH BERRY

"Oh, if that poor child could return here from the grave ..."

SARAH PEMBERTON snapped awake at five o'clock on the morning of February 15th, 1886, to find her niece Elizabeth Berry shaking her.

"Come quick! It's mama — I think she's ... she's dying," Elizabeth said.

Mrs. Pemberton thought that Elizabeth, although a qualified nurse, must be exaggerating. So she was shocked to find her sister, Mary Ann Finley, writhing around in a violent fit. Her face was deeply flushed, as if all her blood had gone to her head, and she was clutching wildly at her bedclothes.

Mrs. Pemberton could hardly believe the sudden change in her sister's condition.

At bedtime the previous evening she had been in good spirits, yet now she was on the brink of death.

Elizabeth ran to fetch the surgeon, Mr. W. H. Sharples, but there was little he could do for the patient, who died shortly after his arrival. He signed the death certificate stating that Mary Ann Finley had died from cerebral haemorrhage.

Mrs. Pemberton was uneasy; not only because of the suddenness of her sister's death but also because of Elizabeth's uncharacteristically caring behaviour. For it was no secret that the ambitious daughter despised her mother and had at one time disowned her.

Mary Ann Finley had never looked beyond her station in life or hankered for finery, whereas Elizabeth had wanted nothing less, developing a driving ambition to better herself in a way that was beyond the scope of her poor drudge of a mother.

Yet when the old lady became sick, Elizabeth had nevertheless given up her post as head nurse at Oldham Workhouse and uncomplainingly sat up with her night after night. Then on February 11th Mrs. Pemberton had received a telegram from Elizabeth, requesting help and saying that her mother was dangerously ill. Mrs. Pemberton had gone immediately to the tiny house in Back Albion Street, Castleton, near Rochdale, where she and her niece had taken turns nursing Mrs. Finley.

Despite the marked improvement in her mother's health, Elizabeth persisted in saying she was "sinking fast," describing a dream she'd had in which Mrs. Pemberton had come to Castleton to bury the patient.

Two further incidents made Mrs. Pemberton uneasy. On the evening before Mary Ann died, Elizabeth offered her some jelly, but after only a few mouthfuls her mother pushed the plate away, complaining that it tasted nasty. Later that night, when Mrs. Pemberton went into her sister's bedroom to say goodnight, she found her niece there rubbing the old lady's eyes although the patient was protesting that they were not sore.

Mrs. Pemberton would remember these incidents, and one day they would be important.

The day after her mother's funeral, Elizabeth Berry, wearing an exquisite silk mourning costume, went to the offices of Joseph Chadderton of the Wesleyan and General Assurance Society. Her mother's life had been insured for £100, an unusually large amount for such a poor woman.

Elizabeth herself had paid the premiums on the policy, but to her surprise Chadderton informed her that the money would not be paid out for three months. Elizabeth explained that she was going to Australia the following week, nursing, so Chadderton waived the regulation and paid her. She then went to the office of Harry Jackson, the agent for the Prudential. Her mother's life was also insured here, and the Prudential paid out £27.6s.

Elizabeth had striven hard to become a fine lady, and to her way of thinking her mother had deserved to die in poverty because she had done nothing to drag herself out of it.

Elizabeth had been born in 1856, and her weaker twin died in early infancy. Their father was killed in the Crimean War, and Elizabeth had never forgiven her mother for replacing him by marrying a weaver, William Finley, who had ill-treated his ready-made family. Elizabeth hated him, refused to call him "father" and let him know that she considered him to be beneath her.

To her relief he found married life and a rebellious step-daughter too much for him and one day he left for good. Thus abandoned, Elizabeth had to leave school as soon as she was old enough, and work alongside her mother in a mill.

But she had glimpsed how better-off people lived and was determined to emulate them. The Crimean War had been devastating, but its aftermath gave her an opportunity to better herself. Until Florence Nightingale made her name in the Crimea, nursing had never been respectable, but it was now considered an honourable way for a young woman to make a career, and Elizabeth trained as a nurse. Since she was both pretty and charming, she was easily accepted by fellow-nurses from better backgrounds.

She also attracted many admirers, one of whom she married. As Mrs. Thomas Berry, wife of a railwayman, she was assured a place higher in society than the one from which she had come and Berry was an indulgent, adoring husband.

A year after their marriage Elizabeth gave birth to a son, Harold. Two years later the couple had a daughter, Edith Annie. They lived at Miles Platting in a much better house than Elizabeth could have dreamed possible, and all would have gone well for them had not Thomas Berry's health failed. He died in 1881 after living like an invalid for two years, and Elizabeth received £70 insurance money.

Fourteen months later her son Harold became ill after a trip to Blackpool, and three days later he died too. Mrs. Berry received £5 insurance money on his death.

Now that she was a widow having to find work, she left her daughter in the care of an aunt and went to the Royal Infirmary in Manchester as a nurse. After completing her training she worked in various private houses, then at Burton-on-Trent Workhouse, and finally in January 1886 she obtained an appointment at Oldham Workhouse.

After her mother's death she might well have intended to go to Australia to nurse, as she had told the insurance agent, but in July she successfully reapplied to Oldham Workhouse for her old job as head nurse, returning to the post at a salary of £25 a year, plus her keep.

During that year she saw little of her daughter, but on December 27th, at the urging of Dr. Patterson, the chief medical officer of the workhouse, she took a holiday. She went to visit Edith, now 11, and stayed with her at Miles Platting for two days. As she was preparing to leave, Edith begged to be allowed to go with her. Elizabeth compromised and told her she could come for a few days' holiday, but only on the condition that she brought her best friend Beatrice Hall with her for company. Edith delightedly agreed.

Beatrice joined the Berrys on the train to Oldham, and for the first two days the girls enjoyed themselves running about the workhouse and gardens. Then on the morning of January 1st, 1887, Edith was too ill to eat breakfast and went to find her mother.

Later Beatrice found Edith with her mother in the nurse's sitting-room, being violently sick, and heard Mrs. Berry, tumbler in hand, tell her, "Drink this darling." But Edith, turning her face away with a grimace, protested tearfully, "Oh, mama, I cannot drink it."

"Oh, drink it, love, it will make you better," coaxed her mother, pressing the glass to her lips. Then, seeing Beatrice at the door, Elizabeth told her she had to play on her own that day as Edith was ill and going to bed.

Mrs. Berry later went to see Dr. Patterson and told him that Edith had been vomiting a lot that morning, bringing up blood. He examined her and made up an astringent mixture of tincture of iron and quinine to ease what he thought must be an upset stomach. But when he saw Edith again that evening, he was disturbed to discover that she was still vomiting. He enquired about the medicine and when Elizabeth explained that her daughter had refused to take it, he advised her to discontinue it. On the morning of January 2nd he was pleased to find Edith much improved and told her mother that he thought she would make a full recovery. To help her on the way he made up a solution of bicarbonate of soda to which he added a further solution of creosote, telling Elizabeth to administer it with milk.

At 9.30 that evening, he again visited the little girl, to find that her illness had taken a sudden, severe turn for the worse. Edith was in agonising pain, her eyes were sunken and he could not feel her pulse. He also noticed that her mouth was red and swollen and there were blisters on her upper lip. He questioned her mother and she told him that earlier that day she had given Edith an orange dipped in sugar. After another examination Patterson concluded that the child had been poisoned, so at 10.30 p.m. he called in Dr. George Robertson of Oldham Royal Infirmary.

Robertson agreed that Edith appeared to have been poisoned, and Patterson made up a solution of bismuth and morphia for her. At 11 a.m. on January 3rd he called to check on her progress, but she was no better, and she died at 5 a.m. the following day.

Dr. Patterson told Mrs. Berry he could not issue the death certificate she requested because he was not sure of the cause of death. Instead, he said he required her permission to make a post-mortem examination. Elizabeth hesitated and then gave her consent.

Dr. Patterson, knowing that a death certificate would be needed in order to claim any insurance money, asked her if Edith had been insured.

"No, not for a penny. I shall have to pay for everything myself," sighed Mrs. Berry. But that was not quite true because Edith was insured for £10. And only a few days earlier Elizabeth had approached a company for a mutual insurance on her own life and her child's, by which £100 would be paid on the death of either, to the survivor. She was under the impression that the proposal had been accepted, but it had not. The paperwork had not been completed.

On January 6th, Dr. Patterson and Robertson, together with Dr. Thomas Harris of the Manchester Royal Infirmary, carried out a post-mortem examination on Edith Annie Berry. The mucous membrane of her stomach and small intestines had marks of blood on them, as did the lining of the gullet, which also had a black and corroded appearance. As the body bore no signs of any natural disease, the doctors concluded that Edith had died from some corrosive poison which might have been administered on the morning of January 1st and then carried off in her vomit, leaving no trace.

Dr. Patterson knew a supply of sulphuric acid was kept locked up in the dispensary, which was next to Mrs. Berry's sitting-room. Although he had the only key to the cupboard, Mrs. Berry had easy access to the dispensary and was often in and out during the course of her duties.

On the pretext of wanting to have a more detailed history of Edith's case, he questioned Elizabeth about what medicines she had given her daughter. Probably sensing she was under suspicion, she claimed that she had given Edith only what he had prescribed, with the exception of a little champagne and ice on January 3rd. She then broached the subject of a death certificate and Dr. Patterson reluctantly made one out stating that the cause of death was acute inflammation of the stomach and bowels.

But the ink was barely dry on the paper before he was on his way to see Chief Inspector Charles Hodgkinson, who called on Mrs. Berry and told her foul play was suspected. She asked, "Why should I kill my darling? I have just doubled the insurance on her."

An inquest was held at the workhouse on January 7th. Mrs. Berry attended, as one newspaper noted, "dressed in fashionable mourning clothes and looking calm, cool and unmoved." But at the end of the first day, when she was about to be taken to the police station, her self control left her. She tearfully asked the court to allow her to remain at the workhouse. The request was granted on the condition she was put under "house arrest." Consequently Dr. Patterson ordered a workhouse resident, Ellen Thompson, to watch her day and night.

When it was realised the evidence was about to become sensational Mrs. Berry, despite her protests, was removed under guard to the Town Hall cells. As she wasn't yet a convicted prisoner she was allowed a flock mattress, a pillow and bed covering.

On January 20th the inquest ended with a verdict of wilful murder against Elizabeth Berry, who fainted as she was arrested. Meanwhile little Edith Berry was quietly buried at Chadderton Cemetery. Her mother paid for the funeral but was refused permission to attend and there were only five mourners.

On January 22nd Elizabeth Berry was brought before Oldham magistrates who concluded that as there was no established motive for the crime there was no case to answer, so they dismissed the charge against her.

But the coroner's warrant of wilful murder was none-theless upheld and on February 21st, 31-year-old Elizabeth Berry went on trial before Mr. Justice Hawkins at Liverpool Assizes.

Sobbing bitterly, Mrs. Ann Sanderson, 68, told the court that Edith, her great-niece, had lived with her for five years, until December 29th, 1886. Mrs. Berry had called from time to time, she said, and had paid £13 a year for

Edith's keep. On December 29th, when Edith left to spend a few days with her mother, she had been in the best of health, and a day before being taken ill had written to Mrs. Sanderson saying she was having a good time.

Then on January 3rd, the witness had received a telegram from Elizabeth which read, "Come at once, Edith is dying."

Mrs. Sanderson's husband had gone immediately to the workhouse where Elizabeth said that Edith was suffering from stoppage of the bowels due to eating cheese and apple pie on New Year's Eve.

But, said Mrs. Sanderson, in all the time she had looked after Edith the child had never suffered from constipation.

Beatrice Hall, Edith Berry's schoolfriend, told the court about the Christmas holiday she had spent at Oldham Workhouse. For the first day or so she and Edith had played happily and had always eaten together. On the evening of December 31st — the day before Edith became ill — they both enjoyed a hearty supper and neither complained of feeling sick.

However, the following morning at about 10 o'clock Edith — who had not been out of her company — was so ill she could not eat breakfast.

Under cross-examination Beatrice said that Mrs. Berry was always loving towards Edith.

Harry Jackson, the Prudential agent, said he had known Mrs. Berry since she went to see him in April 1886 about insuring her own and Edith's life. She had told him she wanted to take out an insurance policy for £100 to safeguard her daughter's future because she intended remarrying.

Dr. Patterson then gave evidence about the last four days of Edith Berry's life and the findings of the post-mortem examination. Questioned about the child's improvement on the morning of Sunday, January 2nd, and her sudden decline that evening, he said that he was certain she had been poisoned a second time. He had not given her an antidote because he had no means of knowing which poison had been given — sulphuric acid, he later surmised. His main concern at the time was to relieve her suffering by stopping the pain and vomiting. Even if he had known the poison, nothing could have been done because by then it had taken too great a hold on the body.

Mr. James Cottingham, defending, asked why there were no traces of sulphuric acid in the child's stomach, and Patterson replied that it did not necessarily follow that evidence of the poison would be found in the stomach as it would have been quickly ejected during vomiting.

Mr. Cottingham wondered why, if sulphuric acid burnt so badly, Edith hadn't spat it out immediately instead of swallowing it. Dr. Patterson had no explanation.

Dr. Robertson and Dr. Harris then gave evidence, agreeing with Dr. Patterson's findings.

While the trial continued, newspapers were delving into Mrs. Berry's past. Gossip had it that her husband Thomas was hardly cold in his grave before she was courting a young curate, whom she'd threatened to sue for breach of promise when he refused to marry her. The curate had subsequently paid her £150 to settle the matter.

Mrs. Berry was also reported to have boasted at Oldham Workhouse that she had a lover, a widower of means living at Derby, but he wouldn't marry her until his son came of age.

In Castleton, a neighbour of Mrs. Berry's deceased mother told a reporter that Mrs. Finley had adored her daughter and always gave her whatever she could so that Elizabeth could look nice. But when the old lady was out of work and had to pawn some of her clothes to buy tea, the neighbour saw Mrs. Berry bring out £11 which she put straight back in her purse without giving her mother a penny.

The same neighbour also recalled Mrs. Finley's account of a visit she had made to her daughter's home prior to her grandson's christening. Mrs. Finley had been horrified to find her daughter about to put the baby on the fire and stopped her in the nick of time.

This story was made much of because it was felt to reveal Mrs. Berry's murderous instincts, but the incident could have been the result of post-natal depression which thousands of women suffer.

Meanwhile William Finley, Mrs. Berry's stepfather, was in Manchester and talking freely about his stepdaughter to all who would stand him a pint. He had little to say in her favour.

"I tell you," he growled as he gulped his beer, "if I'd lived under the same roof with her much longer I reckon I'd have been a goner for sure."

All these stories, some true, many exaggerated, did nothing to help Mrs. Berry's case. But her defence counsel had found a medical witness to challenge Dr. Patterson's findings.

William Thompson, an analytical chemist, stated that if sulphuric acid had been administered, he would have expected to find traces of it in the stomach, despite violent purging, weeks afterwards. He also said that creosote, which Dr. Patterson had prescribed for Edith, contained carbolic acid and this could have been responsible for blistering the skin around her mouth. And the black mark in her throat could have been caused by tincture of iron, which Dr. Patterson had also prescribed.

Mr. Cottingham told the jury that as no trace of poison had been found in the child's body, the prosecution's claim that Edith Berry had died under suspicious circumstances was highly dubious, especially as they had failed to establish a motive.

"After all, what motive could possibly transform a mother into a monster?" he asked.

He said there was no evidence that Mrs. Berry needed the insurance money or that she resented the expense of keeping her daughter. She had a good salary and a large sum in the bank.

The defence counsel went on to ask why, if Dr. Patterson knew Edith had been poisoned, had he prescribed bismuth and morphia which would prevent vomiting — the very thing which would rid the body of poison. After all, he could not have been absolutely certain the child was beyond help — he was not God! Why had he not communicated his suspicions to the police earlier? Why had he signed a death certificate stating natural causes, when he was certain the child had been poisoned?

"A man like Patterson is to be judged on his acts rather than his words," Mr. Cottingham told the jury.

Ann Dillon, a workhouse inmate, had made a statement that she had seen the mother and daughter alone in the dispensary before Edith was taken ill, but Mr. Cottingham reminded the jury that this evidence was uncorroborated. Alice Alcock, another workhouse inmate, had been in the kitchen all that morning with the door wide open, but she had seen no-one go into the dispensary. And Beatrice Hall had sworn that Edith had been with her all morning until she became ill.

"Oh, if that poor child could return here from the grave, would she call vengeance down upon this woman?" Mr. Cottingham cried, pointing dramatically at his client. "Or would she proclaim the innocence of a mother who had always been so loving and anxious for her welfare?"

Summing-up, Mr. Justice Hawkins told the jury: "People in all ages have been found inhuman enough to take the lives of their little children, and then for the most paltry considerations. Mrs. Berry being the child's mother must not duly influence you."

After only 10 minutes' deliberation the jury brought in a verdict of guilty. The judge asked Mrs. Berry if she had anything to say and in a quiet, dignified voice she replied, "I may be found guilty, but the whole world cannot make me guilty."

Sentenced to death, she was removed from the dock and taken to Walton Prison to await execution.

During her trial newspapers had also been reporting a coroner's inquest held at the Blue Pits Inn at Castleton. This inquiry was into the death of Mrs. Finley, Elizabeth Berry's mother. After Mrs. Berry had been charged with

Edith's murder, the Home Secretary had granted an order for the exhumation of Mrs. Finley's body, and this had prompted speculation about multiple murder. How had Mrs. Berry's husband died? And her son?

Having testified at Elizabeth Berry's trial, Dr. Harris told the inquest that on February 3rd, 1887, he examined Mrs. Finley's body at Moston Cemetery, near Manchester, and failed to find any natural disease that would account for her death. The body, which was wrapped in newspaper instead of a shroud, was very decomposed, but the stomach was not destroyed. This, together with other organs, had been sent for analysis to Dr. Paul in Liverpool.

Dr. Paul, lecturer in medical jurispudence at the University College in Liverpool, told the court that he had found a substance in the stomach and intestines which he believed might be atropia, a poisonous alkaline in deadly nightshade which could cause death by destroying the nervous system.

Mr. Sharples testified that he had begun treating Mrs. Finley on January 27th, 1886, for a minor nervous complaint. Despite his treatment her health had rapidly deteriorated and she had died during a violent fit.

Although at the time he had not considered the death to be suspicious and had signed a certificate giving the cause as cerebral haemorrhage, he told the coroner that having heard Dr. Paul's evidence he now believed that she had died from atropin poisoning. All her symptoms — flushed face, quick pulse and irregular movements of the muscles — were consistent with the effects of that poison.

John Taylor, a chemist of Yorkshire Street, Rochdale, told the court that on February 9th, 1886, a woman of about 30 had come into his shop for sulphate of atropia for dropping into eyes. She had signed the poisons book as Ellen Sanders, workhouse nurse. Three days later she returned for a further supply, claiming to have knocked over the first bottle.

As Taylor was preparing the mixture she asked him to make her a double amount to save her coming back for more.

William Lawson, Master of Oldham Workhouse, compared the signature in Taylor's poisons book with known specimens of Mrs. Berry's signature and declared them to be very similar.

Sarah Pemberton, the deceased's sister, agreed with the dead woman's neighbours who testified that Mrs. Finley's health had worsened after her daughter arrived to look after her. Death had been startlingly sudden, and they had all seen Mrs. Berry administer medicine which the old lady described as "tasting worse than poison."

Mrs. Berry was neither present nor represented at the inquest. And although the cause of Mrs. Finley's death appeared suspect, the evidence of poisoning was by no means conclusive. Whoever had bought poison from John Taylor had left a signature in the poisons book which could only be said to be very like Mrs. Berry's writing. Yet there were many similarities between Mrs. Finley's death and Edith's. Both had been taken ill suddenly, both had shown symptoms of poisoning, both partially recovered, relapsed and died. And both had been nursed in their last hours by Mrs. Berry.

On February 28th, 1887, the jury — doubtless influenced by the outcome of the trial which had ended two days earlier — unanimously returned a verdict of wilful murder against Elizabeth Berry.

As she was already awaiting execution, no further action was taken. In the condemned cell she continued to protest her innocence accusing Dr. Patterson of poisoning her daughter with his medicines.

Her solicitor, Joseph Whittaker, launched a petition for a reprieve, but although it was signed by many influential Oldham residents, the majority of the public vehemently opposed mercy.

Mr. Whittaker therefore decided to cut his losses and salvage what he could for himself, so he applied to Oldham magistrates saying that Mrs. Berry was in debt to him for his services. In order to recoup his out-of-pocket expenses he wanted all the possessions she had left at the workhouse.

From the death cell Mrs. Berry responded on March 7th, 1887, with a letter to the Guardians of Oldham Workhouse.

"Dear Sirs, you will know that my clothing, together with other articles are still at the workhouse. These things Mr. Whittaker wishes me to give to him on the pleas that he has not been sufficiently paid for my defence. Mr. Whittaker has received from me £64. In addition to this sum he has my watch and chain which are valued at £14. I have left every other article that belongs to me to Mr. George Robinson to dispose of according to my instructions. He has promised me to erect a stone over the grave of my darling (Edith Annie), and for this I feel exceedingly grateful. I appeal to you that none be allowed to remove a single article belonging to me from the workhouse, except Mr. Robinson. And a word with regard to myself. I am very sad, but at peace and in full submission to God. I think I must have loved my dear ones amiss since God, either in His mercy or His jealousy, has removed them."

Robinson was a young man serving his articles with Mr. Whitaker. He had befriended Mrs. Berry in prison, and her letter now placed him in an invidious position.

Meanwhile the law took its course. Wearing a black silk dress and saying repeatedly "May God forgive Dr. Patterson," Elizabeth Berry went to the gallows at 8 a.m. on Monday, March 14th, 1887, to become the first person to be executed at Walton Prison — Liverpool's executions had previously taken place at Kirkdale Gaol. She was hanged by her namesake, James Berry.

Afterwards, Mrs. Berry's clothes were auctioned off. One of the items under the hammer was a beautiful ruby red silk ball-gown she had bought at an exclusive dress shop in Manchester in readiness for the high life she hoped would one day be hers. It was sold for £7 to a waxwork exhibition in Lime Street, Liverpool. There, for the next 36 years until the exhibition was finally dismantled in 1923, the garment rotted slowly away in a damp cellar, surrounded not by ballroom elegance but by effigies of notorious killers and madmen like Dr. Palmer and Charlie Peace.

What would a jury make of Elizabeth Berry's case today? Although several of her nearest and dearest had died suspiciously suddenly, to her benefit through insurance, the evidence of poisoning was based only on medical opinion. Not a particle of poison was identified, and had she been tried in our own times she might well have been acquitted . . . or forensic analysis might have traced poison. She would certainly have been spared the prejudicial press publicity which could not have failed to influence her trial's jury, and which today would put any editor in the dock for contempt of court.

So was Elizabeth Berry guilty? Despite the substantial circumstantial evidence against her, justice might have been best served by the Scottish verdict, "Not proven."

11

YOU WON'T CRY MURDER IN ANOTHER MINUTE

A New Brighton tragedy

FELIX SPICER was desperate. The 60-year-old rigger was beside himself with rage. "Let me in, Mary, let me in!" he shouted, hammering with his fist on the locked door.

But Mary Palin, 33, had no intention of allowing her common-law husband into the New Brighton eating house where she was living.

Months prior to that night of Saturday, May 24th, 1890, the pair had quarrelled violently, and she was not about to forgive and forget. "Goodnight, Spicer!" she shouted through the bolted door.

The old man sighed heavily. "All right, girl, goodnight." Then he shuffled away into the darkness.

Mary Palin turned her face into her pillow and tried to sleep. Her mind kept going over and over her unhappy life.

Seventeen years earlier Mary, then 16, had been lured away from home with the promise of marriage. But although she had borne Spicer seven children, he had always refused to marry her. He had laughed in her face after the birth of their first child, when she begged him to make her his wife, and she had hated him ever since.

It was not their only problem. The couple kept an eating house in the Cheshire resort's Bickley Parade, and a lodging house in Richmond Street, but a few years earlier the business had run into difficulties. As an expediency, the enterprise had been put in Mary's name. But while Mary was away in Liverpool, Spicer had taken money from the shop. When she discovered this she had ordered him not to interfere in the business again.

In retaliation, Spicer had written to the agents of the property, Wright, Beckett and Co., informing them that Mary was not his wife. When she learnt of this she was so upset that she refused to live with him any more. He was now forced to lodge with their children at the Richmond Street house while she remained at the eating house on Bickley Parade.

Spicer had tried to effect a reconciliation, but Mary would have none of it, telling him firmly, "The gallows before another night under the same roof with you."

Knowing he was violent, with an ungovernable temper, she feared what he might do if she kept refusing to go back with him, and it was this fear which kept her awake into the small hours of the morning. She was still awake at 2.30 a.m. when she heard the smashing of glass.

Her heart thumping, she sat up and lit a candle.

Spicer put his hand through the broken window pane and felt about the door for the key.

Shrieking "Murder! Murder!" at the top of her voice, Mary jumped out of bed and quickly pulled on a dress. Failing to open the door, Spicer made another attack on the window.

Mary rushed to the door to get out, but Spicer blocked her way. The next thing she knew, he was trying to put a handkerchief, smelling strongly of brandy, over her mouth. Finding that her struggling hampered him, he took a knife from his breast-pocket — a knife he had bought for fourpence, saying it could "settle all the throats in New Brighton."

"You wretch!" he shouted. "You won't cry murder in another minute when I have done with you!"

As they struggled for the knife, Mary gripped the blade. Then she managed to knock it out of his hand and break away.

Retrieving the knife, Spicer followed her out of the house, chasing her along Victoria Road to Bailey's grocery shop, and then to the cabmen's shelter.

Awakened by the noise, John Bailey came to his door at 4 Victoria Road, and called out to Spicer to stop. The only response was a torrent of abuse.

Not knowing what else to do, Bailey shouted to Mary to run to his shop.

Mr. Francis Storey, of 3 Victoria Road, had also witnessed the fracas and now came to Mary's aid. She begged him to follow Spicer, "or he'll do something to the children."

Storey hurried to Dr. Ross's house and then with Constables Jones and Potts, he went to Spicer's home in Richmond Street.

Spicer immediately opened the door to them. He admitted assaulting Mary and was arrested and taken away.

Remembering Mary's warning about the children, Storey and PC Potts hurried upstairs.

In the first bedroom they found the three girls sleeping peacefully. But the second bedroom was a different story. The bed shared by four-year-old Henry and William, 14, was such a scene of carnage that it was at first hard to tell the blood-soaked sheets from the two dead children. The boys' heads were almost completely severed from their bodies.

From the positions of the bodies and the way the bedclothes were disarranged, Dr. Ross thought the children must have struggled before they were slain. Both had been dead for about an hour before Ross saw them.

Superintendent Hindley examined the house but found no blood anywhere else. He took possession of a plank of wood with which the window of the shop on Bickley Parade had been smashed. It appeared to have been grasped by bloody hands.

Spicer's hands were examined and were seen to have

been recently washed, leaving a tidemark of blood round each wrist. But there were no scratches or cuts on them.

William Foulkes Lowe, the public analyst of Chester, was handed items including an old blue pilot-cloth coat, saturated with blood that was still wet.

Another parcel for his examination contained a black worsted coat which had bloodstains on both sleeves, and on the inside breast-pocket where Spicer had kept the knife.

Superintendent Hindley had seen a mark on the boys' bed which he supposed had been made by someone kneeling there and leaving a bloody imprint.

Spicer claimed that all this blood came from his attack on his wife, but her injuries were too superficial to have produced so much gore.

The analyst also received a short wood-handled knife, with a four-inch blade. This had been found concealed in the flue of the Richmond Street lodging house and it was believed to be the murder weapon.

Charged with his sons' murder. Felix Spicer pleaded not guilty when he appeared at Chester Assizes on Thursday, July 31st, 1890, before Mr. Justice Stephen.

Mrs. Fraser, a servant at the Richmond Street lodging house, told the court that on May 24th, the day prior to the murders, Spicer had told her that four lodgers were expected and that he wanted his three girls and two boys to sleep in one room.

However, she did not put the boys and girls in the same room, but allowed Henry and William to sleep in a separate room as usual. The occupants of the lodging house that night were the five children, two servants, including Mrs. Fraser, a lodger named Short, and Spicer himself.

Spicer did not go to bed, but told Mrs. Fraser he would lie on the sofa and await the arrival of the four expected lodgers.

At about three o'clock in the morning Mrs. Fraser had heard a cry from the boys' bedroom and the sound of shuffling feet, but thought it nothing extraordinary and went back to sleep.

She now wept as she said she might have saved the two boys if she had investigated the disturbance, because she now realised it was then that they were being murdered.

It was alleged that Spicer, covered in his children's blood, had subsequently left the house to carry out his unsuccessful attack on Mary.

Mr. Wood, defending, told the jury that Spicer admitted assaulting Mary Palin, but denied his sons' murder, an act which would have been unnatural and contrary to his previous kind treatment of his children.

The defence claimed that the blood on Spicer's clothes had fallen from Mary Palin, when her face and hands were cut.

No defence witnesses were called, and in conclusion Mr. Wood submitted that if the jury believed that Spicer had been responsible for his sons' deaths he should be convicted only of manslaughter in a fit of insanity.

Summing-up, the judge said there was no evidence of insanity and there could be no manslaughter verdict. Spicer had either committed the murders or he was innocent.

After a brief retirement the jury returned to find Spicer guilty and he was sentenced to death.

Before leaving the condemned cell at Knutsford Gaol for his execution on Friday, August 22nd, 1890, he told the prison chaplain that he must have been mad because he did not remember going upstairs to his sons' bedroom.

"I forgive Mary Ann Palin, and hope she and the children will prosper," he added.

Facing his death calmly, he said only "Good morning, gentlemen," as he stood on the scaffold. Berry, the executioner, was to remark later that it was the quickest execution he had ever performed.

Why had Felix Spicer refused to marry Mary Palin? The mystery was solved shortly after his hanging. A native of London, the son of a Tower Street wine merchant, he had married at an early age, but had left his wife on finding her unfaithful and had lived apart from her ever since.

He had gone to the scaffold unaware that she had been dead for many years.

12

THE MACCLESFIELD CANAL MURDER

"You have only two sons, and one must soon be led to the gallows to die"

IT SEEMED an odd place to leave a shopping basket, in the mud by the towpath of Cheshire's Macclesfield Canal. Blacksmith Joe Jackson, hurrying along at noon on Saturday, March 24th, 1877, stopped in his tracks on seeing the basket and put it on a nearby wall in case its owner came back to look for it.

Then as he turned to continue on his way he glanced and saw something floating in the canal near Hollins Bridge. At first he thought it was a bundle of rags, but on closer inspection he was startled to see a hand and an arm.

Striding into the water, he hauled out a young girl. Her body was still warm so he picked her up and ran with her to the nearby Railway View Inn.

But it was too late. The child was dead. Jackson assumed she must have fallen into the canal and drowned, but as her hair was gently smoothed from her face he was shocked to see blood and some deep cuts ...

Meanwhile, in her terraced house in Fence Street, Macclesfield, Mrs. Emily Halton was beginning to worry. Her eight-year-old daughter Mary Ann had set out at 10.30 that morning to collect her mother's wages from Bamford's silk mill in nearby Sutton. It was now dinner-time, and she still hadn't returned. Had she met a friend, got chatting and forgotten the time?

Her mother's instinct told her this was not the case, and she was overwhelmed by a feeling of dread. Recently widowed, Mrs. Halton had become both mother and father to her little girl, working full-time as a spinner at the mill to support them both.

The hours were long and the pay low, and Mrs. Halton's sole consolation was Mary Ann, her only child.

It was to her that Mrs. Halton often entrusted the responsibility of collecting her weekly wage of 12s 3d from the mill on Saturday morning. Mary Ann, proudly wearing the new straw hat she'd recently been given for her birthday and with her mother's brown purse in her hand, had left the house on the errand, promising to return within the hour. Now, when two o'clock came and there was still no sign of her, Mrs. Halton became frantic and went out to look for her.

At the mill she saw the manager, Mr. Robinson, who told her that Mary Ann had collected her wages that morning. He had watched as the child carefully counted the money before putting it into a small brown purse with a brass snap. She'd then wrapped the purse in a handkerchief and put it in the pocket of her dress for safety. It was about 10.50 a.m. when she left, saying she was going straight home.

When Mrs. Halton told him she hadn't seen Mary Ann, Robinson became concerned. "Then there is some mystery over your money," he said, telling her of a disturbing incident which had occurred some 30 minutes before Mary Ann's arrival at the mill. At 10.15 he had been in his office when Sam Goodwin, a local lad, had come in with a note, supposedly from Mrs. Halton.

The manager now read the note out to her: *"Mr. Robinson, pleas to pay the bearer my wages as my daughter is sick in bed and can't come. Wrap it up in paper with as string so as he will not lose it, and oblige yours: E. Halton, 60, Fence Street."*

The note was written in pencil, in a large, somewhat

masculine hand. Robinson, knowing that Mrs. Halton could neither read nor write, refused the request and the boy had left.

Finding out where young Goodwin lived, Mrs. Halton hurried to see him. He told her that at about 10 o'clock that morning he and two friends, Harry Gosling and George Whittaker, were standing on the corner of Waller Street when a man carrying a brown basket with a broken lid came up to them. The man inquired if Bamford's Mill was in that street and when they said it was, he asked Goodwin to take a note to the mill's manager for him.

The boy did so. But when he returned empty handed, the man had looked disappointed and had hurried away down Mill Lane.

Asked to describe him, the boy said he was young, puny and very short — hardly more than a dwarf. To Mrs. Halton this sounded like 23-year-old Harry Leigh, the step-son of her next-door neighbour and closest friend, Mrs. Ann Leigh. Harry was slightly built and barely 4ft 9ins tall. He was also something of a drunkard and a layabout, but Mary Ann knew him well enough to have gone with him had he asked her.

Mrs. Halton recalled that she had been in Mrs. Leigh's house the previous afternoon. During their conversation she had told her friend, "I've not got my money tonight. I'll have to send my little girl just after ten-thirty tomorrow morning to Bamford's Mill." Harry had been the only other person in the room and would have overheard her.

Having married three months earlier, he now lived in Parsonage Street, and it was 3 p.m. when Mrs. Halton arrived at his home. Leigh was in the kitchen, eating his dinner. Calling him outside, Mrs. Halton told him she was seeking her daughter who had disappeared while on an errand to collect her wages. The distraught mother told Leigh that she knew he had sent a boy to the mill with a note, forged in her name, asking for her money.

Leigh looked at her blankly, saying he knew nothing of any note or the whereabouts of Mary Ann.

Mrs. Halton didn't believe him. "Never mind the money!" she screamed. "Where's my child?"

When Leigh repeated that he knew nothing Mrs. Halton threatened to send for the police.

"I would if I was you," Leigh challenged her, and with that she ran straight to the police station. As the desk sergeant listened to her story he realised that the description she gave of her missing daughter matched that of the child who had been found in the canal earlier that day.

Dr. Rushton had by this time examined the girl's body, concluding that the bruises and scratches on her face were due to her having been gripped around the mouth before being put, or having fallen, into the canal where she had drowned. The tops of her arms were also badly bruised, possibly from being held very tightly. She had not been sexually assaulted.

After identifying her daughter's body Mrs. Halton told the police of her suspicions about Harry Leigh. The police hadn't found a purse with Mary Ann, but Mrs. Halton told them her daughter had put it in the pocket of her dress. Officers re-examined the child's clothes and found that her dress pocket had been ripped away.

At 5 p.m. Inspector Swindells led officers to Leigh's house. His wife Lizzie said that as soon as Mrs. Halton left he had barricaded himself in the outside privy, and he was still there. When Leigh refused to come out, Swindells interviewed him through the locked door. Leigh repeated that he knew nothing of the forged note or Mary Ann's disappearance.

Noting that the news of her death didn't seem to surprise the suspect at all, Swindells asked him to account for his movements that morning. Leigh said he had been working at Briar's Mill in Bollington, a village a few miles from Macclesfield. Swindells, having as yet no firm evidence against the suspect, left to continue his inquiries.

At Bollington he questioned the foreman at the mill where Leigh worked as a weaver. The foreman said that

Leigh hadn't been to the mill for the past fortnight.

At 7p.m. Swindells went back to Parsonage Street to find Leigh still locked in the privy. When he told Mrs. Leigh that her husband hadn't been going to work, she said she thought he'd been working, as he'd left the house each morning at his usual time.

Swindells realised that to maintain this deception Leigh would need money to pass off as his wages, so he had a motive for robbery.

When Leigh still refused to come out of the privy Swindells ordered his men to break down the door, and the suspect was taken into custody.

Mrs. Leigh told the inspector that when her husband arrived home that afternoon he had given her eight shillings. Her sister, who had been visiting her at the time, remembered how pale he looked, and that his socks were wet.

Searching the house, the police found 3s 9d in the pantry concealed under a broken mug. This, together with the $3\frac{1}{2}$d found on Leigh, what he had spent at a pub and the sum he had later given his wife made up the precise amount Mary Ann had received at the mill — 12s 3d.

Charged with the girl's murder, Leigh replied: "I know nothing about it."

As the news spread Mrs. Charlotte Massey came forward to report that between 10.30 and 11 a.m. on the day of the murder she had seen a man with a brown basket in his hand leaning against the wall of the Wheat Sheaf public house. The inn commanded a good view of the entrance to Bamford's Mill. She first noticed him, she said, because she wasn't sure if he was a child or a small man.

Other witnesses remembered seeing Mary Ann after she left Bamford's Mill. Esther Moore said she saw the child walking along Mill Lane with a small, dark-haired man who was about a yard in front of her. They had then turned into Windmill Street, which led to the canal. The man was carrying a brown basket.

Thirteen-year-old George Day, who also knew Mary Ann, said he too had seen her that morning with a very short, dark-haired man walking towards the canal.

Emma Owen, a servant employed at "The Woodlands" in Sutton, told the police that at 11.45 that morning she was cleaning the front windows — which looked out onto the canal — when she noticed either a boy or a small man and a young child walking together along the towpath. They were carrying something between them which they swung about. It looked like a basket.

The girl wore a straw hat, similar to the one Mary Ann was known to have been wearing. As Emma watched the two walked behind a wall, and were then hidden from view. About 15 minutes later Mary Ann's body had been fished out of the canal some 50 yards from this spot.

At the police station Charlotte Massey, Esther Moore, George Day and Emma Owen each identified Harry Leigh as the man they had seen that morning. Sam Goodwin and his two friends were also positive that Leigh was the man who had given them the note to deliver to Bamford Mill.

Nearly all the witnesses remembered that Leigh had been carrying a brown basket, which some recalled had a broken lid fastened on with copper wire. Such a basket had been found near the spot where Mary Ann had drowned, but Leigh's wife did not recognise it. Then Charlie Wright, an 11-year-old schoolboy from Bollington, came forward to clear up that mystery.

He said that at 8.30 on the morning of the murder he had been on his way to school at Macclesfield when he inadvertently left his brown basket on a platform at Bollington Station. The basket contained a plate-custard which his mother had wanted him to deliver to an aunt in Macclesfield.

Taken to Macclesfield police station, the boy instantly recognised the basket found on the canal towpath as his because of its broken lid, which his mother had tied on with copper wire. The plate-custard had gone, but a number of pencils had been found in the basket. And the note forged in Mrs. Halton's name had been written in pencil . . .

Furthermore, a pencil-holder found on Leigh when he was arrested was identified by Mrs. Halton as Mary Ann's.

On March 28th Mary Ann was buried in Macclesfield Cemetery. The whole town came to a standstill as people crowded into the street to watch the cortège pass, and many shops closed as a mark of respect. At the cemetery Mrs. Halton, distraught with grief, wept uncontrollably throughout the ceremony. A day or so later the Mayor of Macclesfield launched an appeal fund for the widow, and the public responded generously.

In custody, Leigh at first appeared indifferent to his predicament, continuing to eat and sleep as if nothing troubled him. But as the evidence mounted against him he became dejected.

At 10.30 p.m. on March 31st Superintendent Sheasby called on Superintendent Dale at Macclesfield police station and asked to see Leigh, with a view to questioning him further about the pencil-holder. When the officers entered Leigh's cell they heard a gurgling noise and found that he was unable to speak. He had made a noose from the silk handkerchief he wore around his neck, pulling it so tightly that he had almost strangled himself.

Taking out his knife, Sheasby cut the material from around Leigh's neck, and the prisoner slumped unconscious onto the floor. Dr. Rushton was sent for. Examining Leigh, he said that if he'd been left a few moments longer he would have succeeded in killing himself.

On April 3rd Leigh told Superintendent Dale he wished to make a new statement. He now admitted he hadn't been to work on the morning of the murder.

"I did not like to say where I had been on March 24th," he said, "as it was nothing to my credit. I went to the Spinners' Arms in Bollington before breakfast and left there about 12.30 p.m. In there I met a young man named Jim Wilson with a huckster's cart near the aqueduct.

"I then came along the fields. The next place I stopped

was the Old Ship Inn, Beech Lane. From there I went home and got dinner. I did not leave home again until I was arrested."

The police went at once to the Spinners' Arms and spoke to the landlord, Levi Brown. Neither he nor Jim Wilson remembered seeing Leigh that morning. But at the Old Ship Inn on Beech Lane, about two miles from where Mary Ann's body was found, the landlady told officers that Leigh had come in at about 1 p.m. that day looking pale and anxious.

He had asked for a glass of ale, and after downing it demanded a second and then a third. Noticing how muddy his clogs were, the landlady asked him where he had been. He told her he had just walked all the way from Bollington — "That's why I've such a thirst on me." But she thought he needed a drink because he seemed very upset about something.

On Saturday, April 7th, Harry Leigh was brought before the magistrates, charged with murder and with trying to commit suicide.

"I admit attempting to commit suicide but not the other," he told the court. "I did not see the girl that day."

But for many in Macclesfield the fact that he had attempted suicide confirmed his guilt, and the court was packed. As the proceedings were expected to be lengthy, Leigh was given a chair ... and being so small he nearly disappeared from view the moment he sat down. One spectator shouted out that he should be placed on a chair on the table, so that all could have a good look at him, while another demanded that he be handed over to them to be dealt with. Leigh's only reaction was a contemptuous smile.

He was committed for trial at Chester Assizes, where on July 24th, 1877, he appeared before Mr. Baron Bramwell, pleading "not guilty."

The prosecution claimed that Leigh had killed Mary Ann because she knew him and could therefore identify him as a thief. That was why he had led her to the canal, "a desolate, remote spot."

Mr. Burke Wood, defending, admitted that Leigh had forged the note from Mrs. Halton and had robbed Mary Ann. But he contended that after the robbery the child "in an agony of distress and fear" had run from him, and in doing so had stumbled into the canal and drowned.

The defence counsel said that if the jury accepted this they must bring in a verdict of manslaughter.

How, asked the judge, had Wood come to regard the drowning of the child as a possible act of manslaughter?

The defence counsel said he had in mind a similar case which had recently come before Mr. Justice Lush, who ruled that where a person was attempting to escape from the violence of a man, and in so doing met her death, the charge should be one of manslaughter.

Mr. Marshall, prosecuting, rose to point out that he had defended the man in that particular case. It concerned a woman who, having been violently ill-treated in an upstairs room, fell downstairs in a desperate attempt to escape and was killed.

The judge said he doubted very much whether that case would apply to the one now before the court. If it did, Leigh would not be held responsible for Mary Ann's death and would therefore be entitled to an acquittal.

As the jury retired to consider their verdict, Leigh watched them file into the jury room and didn't take his eyes from the locked door for one second. When they returned 25 minutes later with a guilty verdict he was so shocked that he couldn't speak.

The judge told the jury that it was, in his opinion, the only verdict they could have reached. He added that they must not, however, read anything into the fact that he now declined to make any comment on the case. Nevertheless, it was noted that on sentencing Leigh to hang he omitted the customary phrase, "May the Lord have mercy on your soul."

In Chester Castle awaiting execution, Leigh had a change of heart. Having shown no remorse during his trial, he was now extremely contrite. He admitted that after robbing Mary Ann he had thrown her into the canal and then callously walked away, leaving her to drown. And he also wrote to Mrs. Halton, begging for her forgiveness.

She replied in a dignified letter penned on her behalf by a clergyman, saying she forgave him.

On August 4th Leigh wrote a last letter to his wife Lizzie: *"My dear wife ... O, fool that I was not to have taken heed of my ways till it was too late. O, that I had not forsaken you and that I had lived that I might have smiled at the prospect before me."*

As his letter indicates, he had received a good education. This was partly due to his wealthy grandfather, a Manchester coal-merchant. On leaving school he seemed to have a bright future ahead of him when he became an assistant to the borough surveyor. But an argument over his wages had prompted him to resign, and he had taken a series of low-paid weaving jobs which he doubtless felt were beneath him. Then, at around Christmas, 1876, he had begun taking time off work to go drinking with "undesirables" ...

A week before his execution he wrote a final sad letter to his parents, saying he had not written sooner because he thought they had left Macclesfield — finding living next door to Mrs. Halton very painful, they had moved to Abourhay Street.

"O, dear father," he wrote, *"as you say, you're almost heart-broken. I myself know you cannot be otherwise. You have only two sons, and one must soon be led to the gallows to die, but as I have said repeatedly, it is only what I deserve for having taken the life of a fellow-creature, and having hurried her unwarned into eternity, vile and miserable sinner that I am!"*

Turning to practicalities, he continued: *"And dear father, you say in your letter you don't know whether we shall be permitted to see each other again in this world, but I am glad to inform you that you can visit me on Thursday or Friday next, so I think you had better come on Thursday to avoid being so near the end of the week. And I may say there are only four persons I wish to see, that is, yourself, my mother, my wife and cousin Ellen Goulden. There is no other I wish to see."*

Accompanied by Lizzie, his parents made their final visit to their son on August 9th, when he told them to comfort themselves with the thought that he was resigned to his fate, which he considered a just one.

At 8 p.m. on August 13th, 1877, Harry Leigh was hanged at Chester Castle. He had walked firmly to the scaffold and was seen to place himself on the drop "without a tremor." Marwood, the executioner, after adjusting the rope, stepped behind him and pulled the lever. Leigh died instantly.

The changes in him from the time he was sentenced to death until his execution were not confined to his demeanour. He appeared to become different physically. One man who met him in prison said later that he spoke and acted more like an earnest young schoolteacher than a brutal child-killer.

Some put his alteration down to the fact that for the first time in his adult life Leigh was not drinking, but was eating and sleeping regularly. The tragedy, for both Mary Ann Halton and Harry Leigh, was that he had reformed too late.

13
HORROR AT THE JOLLY CARTER

Martha ran from the pub, a knife blade sticking out of her face

"MURDER! MURDER!" Startled by the piercing scream, 14-year-old William Higgins sat bolt upright in his bed. It was 11.15 p.m. on Monday, May 22nd, 1826, and William, foster-son of the landlord of the Jolly Carter, at Winton, Eccles, near Manchester, had been half-asleep.

A moment earlier Betty Bate, with candle in hand, had come into his room, followed by one of the inn's regular customers, a hawker known only as Alex.

William assumed that Alex had decided to stay the night and Betty was showing him the other bed.

Alex, unaware of William's presence, suddenly grabbed at Betty from behind.

"Be quiet," she giggled, thinking he was making crude advances. For although she was seven months pregnant and soon to be married, Betty Bate was a girl few men could resist.

Even when Alex pushed her onto the floor, Betty still believed he was being amorous. She told him sharply to behave himself or she would mark him for life.

From where he lay, William then saw the glint of a blade flash in the candle-light. Betty also saw it — too late. She managed to cry out twice before the knife sliced through her windpipe.

William, seeing Betty's blood spurt across the floor, cried out in terror. The attacker, now alerted to the boy's presence, turned and lunged at him, forcing him back onto the bed. In another instant Alex would have cut William's throat, but Betty scrambled to her feet and staggered towards the open door. Alex let go of the boy and went after her.

Seizing his chance to escape, William sprang past the man who was finishing off Betty at the bedroom door. Her attacker made a desparate grab for the boy, but William dashed down the stairs, out of the pub and along Worsley Road, his youthful agility keeping him ahead of his pursuer.

At last, breathless and trembling, he plunged into a ditch and crouched there, hoping Alex would not hear his panting. He heard the tramp of feet and then voices, one of them Alex's. Peeping out of his hiding-place, William saw the hawker, now with another man, standing a mere six feet away from him.

"T'lad must have got away," muttered Alex.

"Ay," agreed the other man, "and we'd best away too, 'fore he gets back with the constable."

The two men turned and to William's relief hurried off across a field in the direction of Eccles.

Still too scared to move, the boy wondered if they had also attacked his foster-parents, Joseph and Martha Blears. They had adopted him when he was orphaned two years earlier, treating him as though he were their own son ...

That Monday had begun for the couple just like any other, except that in the morning 48-year-old Joseph Blears had gone to Manchester on business, leaving Martha to look after the inn, with Betty to help. As it was a Monday, business was likely to be slow, so Joseph knew that his wife and Betty could cope until he came back in the evening.

Martha, however, was nervous about his trip because of the large amount of money on the premises. A friendly society met at the inn every week and people knew that the strong-box, containing some £30 and more, was lodged with Blears before being banked. There had also recently been a dinner of the local Orange Society, after which Blears had accepted £25 for safe-keeping. This meant that there was about £55 on the premises — a mammoth sum at a time when the average weekly wage was between three and six shillings a week.

"You'll be as quick as you can, won't you?" said Martha as she helped her husband on with his coat.

"Now, don't take on so, lass, you fret too much. Nothing will happen," he assured her as he set off to walk the five miles into Manchester.

At 5 p.m., a stranger with a Scottish accent had come into the Jolly Carter and ordered bread and cheese and a glass of beer. Half an hour later another Scot, a hawker named Alex, went up to the bar.

Mrs. Blears was reasonably well acquainted with Alex, since he had been a fairly frequent customer for about a year. She knew him by name because Joseph had swapped a canary Alex had taken a fancy to for some stockings. After this the hawker had called regularly during his rounds of the area. But although he was friendly and talkative, very little was known about him except that he came originally from Dumfriesshire in Scotland, and now lived somewhere in Manchester.

As he drank his beer, Alex had asked Martha where her husband was, and on learning that he had gone to Manchester for the day, he asked when he was likely to return. Martha said she didn't know.

Although the two Scotsmen appeared not to know one another, whenever Martha went into the kitchen to get something she could hear them whispering.

Her thoughts turned anxiously to the strong-box and she was relieved when at 8 p.m. the door of the inn flew open and Joseph came in. Tired and dusty from his journey, he sat down by the fire. In a trice, Alex was on his feet, pressing Joseph to have a glass of whisky with him. The landlord didn't feel like drinking, but he didn't wish to seem unsociable, so a whisky was ordered; and after a toast to their mutual good health and happiness, more was bought. The talk that followed was about Joseph's hopes of selling the Jolly Carter for £50. He tended to be boastful and it was because of this that people in the neighbourhood knew about the large sums of money he kept on the premises.

In a corner of the bar sat the Scottish stranger, who didn't join in the conversation but listened intently. Joseph eventually rose to retire. He said goodnight to his customers, but Alex wasn't letting him go. He had had some good luck, he told Blears, and a little money had come his way which he wanted to share. Another whisky was ordered. Joseph wearily thanked Alex, and added water to it from a jug on the table. He put the glass to his lips and knocked it back in one go. Although diluted, it seemed much stronger than the first glass. He tried to get up from the chair and almost fell over, prompting Alex to roar with laughter. Joseph did not want any more, but the Scotsman wouldn't hear of his refusing. A third and a fourth glass were ordered. Soon Joseph was snoring fit to bring down the roof.

Martha saw Alex and the stranger exchange meaningful glances. Then Alex took his own glass, which was still more than half full, across to Joseph. Gently lifting the landlord's head, he put the glass to his mouth and tried to pour the remaining whisky down his throat. "No more, no more," Joseph protested, struggling to his feet and wiping his mouth and whiskers.

Alex apologised and went back to his table. Joseph told Martha to pour him a glass of water from the jug on the table. After drinking it he lay down on the sofa and went to sleep.

From them on, whenever Martha left the room she could hear Alex and the stranger whispering. Uneasy about them, she decided to sit in the bar near her husband in order to watch them more closely.

Young William sat with her, but at 10 o'clock Martha

The Bull's Head in the centre of Manchester where Betty Eckersley met former boy friend Tom Done

Right, the Rochdale Canal in Manchester. Chapter 1

The scene of the murder showing Chipperfield's car and an X marking the spot where Edith Richardson (left) collapsed and died. Below, Whitby in Yorkshire, where the fatal affair began. Chapter 2

People are seen leaving 22 John Bright Street on the day Thomas Farnworth (inset and above) made the horrific discovery in his yard (above). Right, three-year-old Helen Chester. Chapter 3

Left, Howty Brook in Priesty Fields, Congleton, where parts of Ann Smith were found. Chapter 5

Right, Louisa Merrifield. She told an acquaintance that the old lady had died three weeks before her actual death. Chapter 7

The knocker-up was surprised to see a light burning at all hours at 412 Hollins Road, Oldham. Chapter 9

Right, Elizabeth Berry, whose fine ball-gown rotted away in a Liverpool waxwork exhibition. Chapter 10

The Jolly Carter at Winton, near Eccles. Right, a contemporary newspaper illustration showing the blade that had been driven into Martha Blears's face. Chapter 13

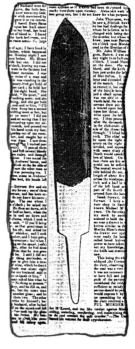

Above, Kate Garrity and right, Jack Griffiths. He used a messenger boy to send threats to his former sweetheart. Chapter 19

Richard Davies Snr. (far left), his sons Richard (left) and George, and their farmhouse home. Chapter 23

THE CREWE MURDER.

THE TRAGEDY ILLUSTRATED.

A body was carried from the canal in Pendleton to the Church Inn (above) in Albert Street. Chapter 24

told him to go to bed. She hoped that the men would get up soon and leave, but they didn't.

At 11 p.m. Alex yawned and announced that it was too late for him to go back to Manchester. He asked Martha if he could have a bed for the night, and the stranger said he would like a room as well, adding, "I never like to go out late from a public house when I have a good deal of money about me."

Alex, glancing at the still snoring landlord, asked Martha if she stayed up with her husband when he was drunk. Martha, unsure of what to say for the best, replied vaguely that sometimes she did and sometimes she didn't. Then she called for Betty Bate to get a room ready, and with candle in hand the servant led the two guests upstairs.

When they had gone, Martha busied herself in the tap-room, clearing up. Suddenly she was startled to hear a scream from the floor above. Grabbing a candle, she was about to run upstairs when she was confronted by the stranger at the door of the tap-room. Without a word, he drew a large knife from his coat and swiped at Martha's throat. Realising he had missed the vital spot, he slashed at the landlady again, but she struggled so violently that he could inflict little more than superficial cuts. Then he forced her to her knees and plunged the knife into her face, stabbing her with such force that the blade penetrated to a depth of four inches through her cheek. There the knife stuck until the attacker pulled the handle off, leaving Martha with the blade sticking out of her face.

At that moment, seeing Alex run out after William, the stranger left Martha and followed to join the pursuit.

Martha stumbled along the passage and out through the front door. William, from his hiding-place in the ditch, saw her come down Worsley Road. Scrambling from his hiding-place, he ran to help her to the home of her niece, Mary Andrews.

Mary took one look at her aunt covered in blood and with a knife sticking out of her face, and promptly fainted. As her husband Richard came to the door, William cried,

"Come quick! They've killed Betty!"

In the bar Joseph Blears woke to hear something strike the wall and some mugs clatter to the floor. He sat up and called out for Martha. After stumbling around the bar for a few minutes, he went into the tap room where he was startled to see a pool of blood on the floor. He was blearily examining it when Richard Andrews appeared at the door, pistol in hand, and told him what had happened.

Instantly sober, Joseph accompanied Andrews up the stairs. Betty Bate lay on the floor of the club-room, her throat a gaping wound and her clothes drenched in blood.

"It was," Blears said later, "one of the most ghastly sights I ever beheld."

Curiously, the police were not called until 6 a.m., so the killers had ample time to escape. Once alerted, however, the police learned that the hawker named Alex was 30-year-old Alexander McKeand, who lived with his mother and sister in Manchester's Quay Street. From the description of his accomplice it seemed that he was McKeand's younger brother, 24-year-old Michael. They were both dealers in linen and tea, but in January that year they had become bankrupt.

The police went to Quay Street and put Mrs. McKeand and her daughter in the workhouse. Then they searched the family's home. Going through Alex McKeand's papers, they found a letter from his girl friend in Ayrshire telling him that he now had a son and begging him to come and see her. The police wondered if that was where he and Michael were now heading.

Officers also learned that the brothers might have been involved in a brutal murder at Milnthorpe, near Kendal, about two years earlier.

A reward of £50 was offered for the two men's capture, and handbills carrying descriptions of the McKeands were distributed to inns and stables by stage coaches travelling to Scotland from Manchester. The police hoped for early results, and they were not disappointed.

At daybreak on Friday, May 26th, blacksmith Richard

Fariday saw a man limp into the small town of Appleby in Westmorland. The man was dirty and unkempt as if he had been sleeping rough, and Fariday realised that he resembled the description of Alexander McKeand, as detailed on a handbill he had been given the day before.

Unsure about tackling a possible murderer alone, Fariday went into the inn and told two of his friends about the suspicious character. In view of the £50 reward for McKeand's capture. Fariday's friends were easily persuaded to help, and they confronted the stranger.

"Hullo, Alex," said Fariday casually strolling up to him. The Scotsman looked at him and smiled resignedly. His capture was simple and undramatic, for he offered no resistance when his hands were tied behind his back. He was then taken into the inn to await the police.

After making certain his prisoner was secure, Fariday, went out alone in search of Michael McKeand, and an hour later he saw another man wearily plodding into Appleby. As the blacksmith approached him, the suspect sensed his purpose and tried to make a run for it. He was no match for Fariday, however, who easily overpowered him and took him to the inn to join his brother.

When the police arrived, they learned that after failing to find William Higgins, the brothers had decided to make for Dumfriesshire where they had relatives. The following morning they'd slept in a thicket, and on the second and third nights they journeyed along lanes and sheep tracks, sleeping in hedges.

They were now taken to Lancaster Castle where Joseph Blears identified them as the men who had been at his inn on the night of Betty Bate's murder. When Michael faced the landlord, he hung his head in shame, but Alex seemed unperturbed.

Pleading not guilty, the brothers appeared before Mr. Justice Park at Lancaster Assizes on August 17th, 1826, charged with Elizabeth Bate's murder.

A surgeon, Mr. John William Garthside, told the court that he had found Betty Bate lying upstairs at the Jolly

Carter. The trail of blood showed that although her windpipe and carotid artery had been severed, she had managed to get to the bedroom door where she was again attacked. Left for dead, she had stumbled across the landing and into the club-room where she collapsed through loss of blood.

The surgeon said he had been unable to perform a caesarian operation which might have saved her baby, as he had been summoned too late.

He then described how he attended to Mrs. Blears, whom he had found sitting at the door of the Jolly Carter with a knife protruding from her face. While he held her head, his assistant managed to extract the blade. Mrs. Blears, he reported, had been ill for a long time afterwards but was now making a full recovery.

Mrs. Sarah Stewart lived at Smithy Door in Manchester and was a dealer in hardware. She told the court that on the Saturday before the murder she had held a sale of hardware and Michael McKeand had helped her by taking down the lots that were sold.

"Amongst the goods on sale were knives of this kind. They are called bread knives," she told the court after examining the blade that had been pulled from Mrs. Bleas's face.

"Michael McKeand sat near the drawer where they were," she recalled, "and he could easily have taken one without me knowing it."

William Britton, the Constable of Eccles, told the court that he believed that Joseph Blears had been the victim of "hocussing" — the clandestine drugging of liquor with laudanum. He surmised that the jug of water on the table had been laced with laudanum.

William Hancock, a surgeon's apprentice, had lodged with Alex McKeand since December, 1825. He testified that at about 4 p.m. on May 22nd, he had been drinking with Alex and Michael in Oldfield Road, Salford. The brothers, hard-up after their recent business failures, asked him if he would go to Wood's liquor vaults at the end of

Oldfield Road to ask the owner, Mrs. Sharples, for the two shillings and sixpence allegedly owed Michael McKeand. Hancock obliged, but the woman angrily told him to get out of her shop.

Before they parted company for the night, Hancock asked the brothers if they were going home and they said they thought not.

A bloodstained handkerchief found in a field near the Jolly Carter was then produced for Hancock to examine.

"I know this handkerchief; it's mine," he told the court. "But Michael had it on Friday or Saturday before the murder."

The defence claimed that the brothers were victims of mistaken identity. But Joseph and Martha Blears and William Higgins had separately and unhesitatingly identified Alex and Michael McKeand as the two men who had been at the inn on the evening of the murder.

The prosecution argued that the brothers, heavily in debt, had decided to rob the Jolly Carter by first incapacitating the landlord and then murdering the two women and the young boy, who could have put up only the mildest opposition.

After deliberating for only two minutes, the jury found the brothers guilty of wilful murder and they were sentenced to hang the following Monday, August 21st, 1826.

In Lancaster Gaol, while denying any involvement in the murder at Milnthorpe, Alex admitted he had murdered Betty Bate, claiming he had been drunk. Michael, however, said that his brother had also attacked Mrs. Blears.

"Oh, God forgive him, he is guilty and well he knows it," cried Alex when he was told of his brother's treachery.

After Alex had murdered Betty Bate he could hardly have had time to attack Mrs. Blears as well as chase William Higgins from the house. Nevertheless, Michael wrote to the judge, asking him to reconsider the case. The request was rejected.

On the morning of the execution, which was attended by Joseph and Martha Blears and William Higgins, a temporary scaffold was erected and two chains were attached to a tree and placed near one another. At 7 a.m., the brothers were brought out, pinioned, and had halters placed round their necks. Then when all was ready the executioner pulled a cap over their faces.

When the drop fell, Alex died instantly but Michael struggled for some time and several spectators fainted.

After hanging for an hour the bodies were cut down and carried into the prison. They were given to surgeons for dissection, Alex being sent to Lancaster Infirmary and Michael to the infirmary in Manchester. So great was the curiosity to see Alex's remains that a crowd forced their way into the dissection-room, putting a stop to the proceedings. To satisfy their curiosity, the chief surgeon had the body put into the yard and "exposed for sometime to the view of all who chose to come and look at it."

To avoid a repetition of this at Manchester, Michael McKeand was put on public display prior to dissection.

William Higgins had within three months witnessed both a murder and a public hanging at close quarters, so did this teach him a lesson? Not really. In later life he was imprisoned in Newgate Gaol for theft and then transported to Australia.

14
THE WARRINGTON POISONINGS

"Bless you, you're in heaven along with your sister, and I shall follow you"

"Arsenic!" Mrs. Alice Arnold stared in dismay at her friend, 30-year-old Mrs. Ellen Heesom. "You say you clean the house with arsenic?"

Ellen nodded. "It's the only way if you're going to get the house really clean." She had moved to Lower Walton near Warrington, Lancashire, in early March 1876. But two weeks later the house was still infested with lice and vermin from the previous tenants, she complained to her friend.

Mrs. Arnold, a former neighbour from nearby Wilderspool, had called to see how she was settling in. Mrs. Heesom went on to describe how she had that morning sprinkled arsenic powder on the bedsteads for lice and round the skirtings for rodents. She then offered some to her friend for the same purpose, but Mrs. Arnold said she would never dare use anything so poisonous around her house.

Mrs. Heesom pointed to a small cupboard. "Oh, if my husband knew I had it, he'd be very cross with me."

Although she referred to 25-year-old Edward Heesom as her husband and called herself Mrs. Heesom, the couple were not in fact married. They had met four years earlier when both were already married. On falling in love with Heesom, a labourer at Wilderspool Brewery, Ellen had left her husband, Andrew Johnson. Taking her daughter Lydia with her, she had set up home with Heesom, and they had subsequently had a child, Elizabeth. Then on their move to Lower Walton, Mrs. Heesom had been excited to discover she was again pregnant.

As the two women chatted about the good news, nine-year-old Sarah Maddock called at the house. She was on her way home from Sunday school and had stopped off to ask after Lydia, Mrs. Heesom's elder daughter. The two girls had attended Sunday school at St. Thomas's Church, Stockton Heath, a village about a mile away, until five months before when Lydia had suddenly become ill.

Since then Sarah had called on her friend each week in the hope that she might be better and they could play out together again. But Sarah saw there was no prospect of that when she entered the kitchen to find Lydia sitting pale and listless in a chair by the fire.

Nobody knew what was wrong with the child, but all agreed that she had little chance of recovery. Even as Sarah chatted to her, Lydia began to be sick. Mrs. Heesom told Sarah to leave, as the visit was upsetting her daughter. Sarah departed promising to call the following Sunday. But by then Lydia was dead.

Mrs. Heesom's grief, however, was lightened by the prospect of a new baby, and on October 5th, 1876, Sarah was born. But the family's troubles were not over. Sarah proved to be a "slow" baby. She was otherwise healthy, however, until October 3rd, 1877, just two days short of her first birthday. On that afternoon she suddenly became desperately ill and died. Dr J. H. Gornall put her death down to a convulsion, and she was buried at St Thomas's Church, Stockton Heath.

On Saturday, November 3rd, 1877, a month after Sarah's death, Mrs. Heesom borrowed a pony and cart from her next door neighbour, Mrs. Elizabeth Moss, and brought her 59-year-old mother Mrs. Lydia Sykes from Warrington to stay with her over the weekend.

The next morning Mrs. Sykes complained of feeling ill. With the rest of the family, however, she had a good lunch of cow's heart stuffed with sage and onions. But 30 minutes later she was violently sick. That evening, as she was no better, Edward Heesom offered to fetch Dr. Charles White, who had attended Mrs. Sykes for the last 20 years. But she told him not to bother as it was nothing and she would soon recover.

Mrs. Heesom was not so certain that it was "nothing." She told her neighbour Mrs. Moss, "I'm afraid Mother is commencing like Lydia," meaning she was showing the same symptoms. To illustrate this she showed Mrs. Moss some of Mrs. Sykes's vomit, light yellow just as Lydia's had been.

Later that night Mrs. Heesom, convinced her mother was dying, begged Mrs. Moss to stay with Mrs. Sykes while she herself went for the doctor. After informing Dr. White of her mother's condition, Mrs. Heesom hurried to tell her two sisters, Mrs. Sarah Ann Whitfield and Mrs. Elizabeth Crompton, of their mother's failing health. Mrs. Crompton returned with her at once to Lower Walton to be present when the physician arrived.

Dr. White found there was little he could do for Mrs. Sykes, apart from relieving her vomiting and diarrhoea, which he was doing when the old lady's husband Robert arrived. He had only just been told of his wife's condition and had come to take her home. Although Mrs. Sykes wanted to return with her husband, Dr. White insisted she was too weak to be moved.

Sykes, at Mrs. Heesom's insistence, stayed overnight and was present when his wife died at eleven o'clock the next morning, November 5th. Just prior to her death she had been seized with violent cramp, and Mrs. Heesom had rubbed her legs in an attempt to ease it.

Sykes called on Dr. White, obtaining a death certificate which stated that his wife had died from exhaustion due to excessive diarrhoea and vomiting.

On Wednesday the 7th an inquest was opened at the

Stag's Head Inn, Lower Walton. The coroner, Mr. T. J. Ridgway, ordered a post-mortem examination.

When Police Constable George Foden went to Mrs. Heesom's home and informed her of this, she said that her mother's body "should not be opened for anyone." Told that the cause of death had to be established, she replied sharply: "Well, if the doctors find anything in her, she has taken it herself."

Foden had not said that poison was suspected, but rumours were circulating.

On November 8th the post-mortem examination was performed by Dr. T. S. Smith at Mrs. Heesom's home. Edward Heesom, who insisted on being present, protested: "It's a curious thing that there should be all this bother when we have got a doctor's certificate."

The contents of Mrs. Sykes's stomach and other organs were sealed in glass jars and sent to Mr. J. Carter Bell, the county analyst, in Manchester. He at once noticed a white sediment at the bottom of the jar containing the stomach. This sediment proved to be arsenious acid, of which there were seven grains — more than sufficient to cause death.

So Mrs. Sykes had been poisoned with arsenic, taken about noon the day before she died.

Superintendent Steen of the Runcorn police, accompanied by the county analyst and Sergeant Levi Bebbington from Stockton Heath police station, visited Mr. and Mrs. Heesom and asked them if they had any arsenic in the house.

"No," the couple replied, "we never had any arsenic in the house in our lives. But you are welcome to look upstairs and down." The three callers took them up on their invitation, but found no arsenic.

As Mrs. Heesom had also lost two children in the last 20 months, the remains of her daughter Sarah were exhumed at St. Thomas's graveyard. The coffin was opened in the tower of the church where Dr. Smith carried out the post-mortem examination. The body's intestines showed no sign of decay, suggesting the presence of arsenic which acts as a preservative.

More sealed jars were sent to the county analyst. He found two grains of arsenic in the stomach: more than enough to kill a baby. In his opinion the poison was administered at about noon on the day Sarah died.

At her inquest at the Saracen's Head, Wilderspool, on January 7th, 1878, Dr. Gornall said he had been summoned by Edward Heesom, who came to his surgery in a very agitated state, saying that Sarah was having fits. When he arrived at the house he found the baby having a convulsion on her mother's lap. He had not attended Sarah before, and Mrs. Heesom told him the child had become ill at noon, having she supposed eaten something indigestible. Realising that Sarah would not live long, Dr. Gornall said he did what he could to relieve her diarrhoea and vomiting, which he thought at the time were due to teething and indigestion. However, he now agreed that arsenic would have the same effect.

The jury decided that Sarah Heesom had died from arsenical poison administered by her parents, and on the following day Superintendent Steen arrested Ellen Heesom at her home, charging her with Sarah's murder. As she tied on her bonnet to leave for Stockton Heath police station, Steen asked her if she had given her daughter any medicine before she died.

"I never gave my child anything but teething powders," she replied.

Steen wanted to know if she had any of the powders left. She said she didn't. "I only got one," she explained, "and a small bottle of cough mixture. I got them the day before the child's death from Mr. Whitby, a chemist in Warrington."

On the way to Stockton Heath police station with Mrs. Heesom, Steen called at Wilderspool Brewery for her husband. Charged with his daughter's murder, Edward Heesom protested, "I was too fond of my children to do anything to them."

Ellen Heesom had handed Steen the bottle of cough

mixture which she claimed to have bought from Mr. Whitby the day before her daughter's death — October 2nd, 1877. But when the chemist examined the residue in the bottle he had a surprise for Steen. He didn't deny the cough medicine was his own preparation, but he said it was a recipe he hadn't used for some months. So Mrs. Heesom could not have bought the mixture when she said she did, and the chemist could not recall selling teething powders to either Mrs. Heesom or her husband.

Steen next questioned Mrs. Elizabeth Moss, who lived next door to Mrs. Heesom and was constantly in and out of her house. She described Mrs. Heesom as a kind and affectionate mother, but added that she drank heavily at times, as did her husband, and she had been deeply troubled about Sarah's "slowness."

Mrs. Moss said that on the afternoon Sarah died Mrs. Heesom had sent her elder girl Elizabeth hurrying in to ask her to come at once. As Mrs. Moss entered the house Sarah was on her mother's lap, working her shoulders and shaking her head as if in great pain. Mrs. Heesom, who appeared very worried, said: "Sarah is exceedingly unwell," adding with a sigh, "I'm afraid she's going like her sister Lydia."

The child then vomited a light yellow fluid streaked with blood. She was so ill that Heesom was sent for and he fetched a doctor. After Sarah's death that evening Heesom had told Mrs. Moss he'd been astounded when the child was taken ill so suddenly, as he had been playing with her in the garden at lunch-time.

Mrs. Moss then recalled the death of Lydia Johnson. The morning before she died — March 26th, 1876 — Mrs. Heesom had told her the child was very ill. When the neighbour went in to see her about 10 a.m. Lydia was sitting on a chair looking very pale and vomiting a fluid similar to that which Mrs. Moss had seen later shortly before Sarah died. Lydia was no better the next morning, and shortly after 4 p.m. Mrs. Moss saw her die in convulsions.

After closing the child's eyes, Mrs. Heesom had told Mrs. Moss, "Mother will go out of her mind because she was not here to see Lydia in her last sickness," hinting that Mrs. Sykes enjoyed watching people die.

On January 14th, 1878, Mrs. Heesom spoke through the cell-door at Stockton Heath police station to Mrs. Bebbington, wife of the sergeant. She said: "If you will get pen, ink and paper I will tell you about my children dying. The day before Lydia died, my mother came to Walton and fed her with bread, butter and tea. About half an hour after she had left, Lydia began to vomit, the fluid being a yellowish colour."

"But why do you think your mother did anything?" asked Mrs. Bebbington.

"If Sarah and Mother died from poison," Mrs. Heesom replied, "Lydia did, for she died the same way. I have never had any poison in my house stronger than paraffin oil, have I, Edward?"

"No," Heesom confirmed.

Mrs. Heesom went on to say that on the day before Sarah died Mrs. Sykes again came to Walton and made a meal of bread and milk for the child. Mrs. Heesom said she had offered to give the food to Sarah, but her mother insisted she go upstairs and make the bed while she fed her. After Mrs. Sykes went home Sarah, like Lydia, became violently ill.

"If anything was given wrong it was something that my mother must have given her," Mrs. Heesom insisted.

But her neighbours Mrs. Moss and Mrs. Owen were sure that Mrs. Sykes had not called the day before Sarah died. They also recalled that the baby had been perfectly well the day before her death.

Mrs. Heesom was not only suggesting her mother had murdered the two children. She went on to claim that Mrs. Sykes had poisoned herself.

"When my mother came to Sarah's funeral," she continued, "she kissed her in her coffin and said, 'Bless you, you're in heaven along with your sister, and I shall follow you.' That night, before she went home, she said, 'I shall be next.' As she said this two or three times the company said, 'You must not think about that yet, you must think of meeting altogether at a wedding before a death again.' But she shook her head, saying, 'We shall not, for you will see.' "

Ellen Heesom and her husband then signed a statement to this effect.

Seeking a motive for the murders, Superintendent Steen learned that Mrs. Sykes and Sarah Heesom had been insured by Mrs. Heesom. Sarah had been insured when she was one month old, and on producing her death certificate Mrs. Heesom had received £1 10s. As Edward Heesom belonged to the Halton Sick and Burial Society he was entitled to money on the death of a child, and he was paid 10 shillings.

About two years prior to her mother's death Mrs. Heesom had, without Mrs. Sykes's knowledge insured her life for a penny a week. However, she and her sister Mrs. Whitfield — the only other person in the family who knew of the policy — had accepted the insurance agent's advice to increase the premium to sixpence a week in the hope of a bigger pay-out. Although both women would benefit from the policy, only Mrs. Heesom paid the premium.

The sisters didn't tell their father about the policy until he obtained his wife's death certificate — which they needed in order to claim the insurance. Mr. Sykes then went with them to the Prudential office in Sankey Street, Warrington, where Mrs. Heesom received £13 which she divided with her sister.

Having ascertained this, Steen went to the Rev. Richard Greenall, vicar of St Thomas's, who kept the books of the church's Sunday School Sick and Burial Club. He recalled that Lydia Johnson had been on the books from May 1874. As the child was sick for 20 weeks her mother had received sick pay for that period. On her daughter's death £5 had been paid to her.

On January 15th, 1878, the case came before Warrington magistrates, with Mr. E. Greenall presiding. When Mrs. Heesom was asked her name she replied, "Ellen Heesom." But when the clerk brusquely requested her to state her lawful name she said, "Ellen Johnson."

A newspaper report described Edward Heesom as "well-favoured of features." Ellen Johnson was reported to have "a most uninviting countenance. She has a dark complexion, has a low forehead, small dark eyes and a nose slightly inclined to turn up to a point. The features are sharp, hard and unprepossessing in the extreme."

At the conclusion of the hearing the couple were sent for trial, charged with the murders of Sarah Heesom and Mrs. Lydia Sykes. The Grand Jury, however, subsequently decided to drop the charges against Heesom who was to remain in custody until the outcome of his partner's trial.

On January 29th, 1878, Lydia Johnson's body was exhumed and a third murder was established. Her remains contained $15\frac{1}{2}$ grains of arsenic.

This suggested that she had been slowly poisoned over a considerable period. Superintendent Steen suspected that her mother had first administered small amounts of arsenic in order to obtain the Sunday school sick pay, finally finishing her off to get the £5 burial payment.

On February 6th, 1878, Mrs. Heesom appeared under her real name of Ellen Johnson at Chester Assizes before Mr. Justice Lush. Dressed in black, she pleaded not guilty to the charge of murdering her daughter Sarah. The law, however, allowed evidence of past deaths to be considered. This meant that the demise of Lydia Johnson and Mrs. Sykes could also be examined.

Mr. J. Carter Bell, the county analyst, told the court that all the arsenic found in the three bodies was white. It could not have been bought from a pharmacist because the chemists who sold arsenic had to mix it with a colour, (usually blue), so that it would not be mistaken for sugar or salt.

So where had Mrs. Heesom obtained her supply? The county analyst suggested an answer. Mrs. Heesom had been employed for several years at Robinson's glass-works in Warrington. Arsenic in its pure white form was used in the manufacture of glass, and at Robinson's it was kept in kegs from which anyone could help themselves.

For the defence, Mr. Swetenham agreed that all three victims had died from arsenic poisoning. But he argued that the case that Mrs. Heesom had administered it amounted to nothing more than suspicion. Hadn't she shown great concern for Sarah when she became ill, and hadn't she quickly sent for a doctor? Would she have done this had she wanted the child to die — especially if she had used arsenic, which could be detected? There was no proof that she had taken arsenic from the glass-works. But even if she had kept some in the house, mightn't little Sarah have inadvertently got hold of it?

There was another adult in the house (the defence counsel did not mention Edward Heesom by name) with equal opportunity and motive for giving poison to Sarah.

At this point the prosecution interrupted to remind the court that Mrs. Heesom had effected all the insurance policies on the three dead people and had paid for them herself.

Summing-up, Mr. Justice Lush reminded the jury that the baby Sarah couldn't walk, so it was unlikely that she would have taken the arsenic herself. It must therefore have been given to her, probably in her food. The defence had suggested that another adult in the house, other than Mrs. Heesom, could have given the child poison. But Edward Heesom, except at meal times and at night, was away from home working at the brewery.

Furthermore, it was known that Mrs. Heesom had been anxious to hide the arsenic from him, as Mrs. Arnold had testified, because he would be angry if he knew she had it.

Finally, said the judge, there was no evidence that Mrs. Sykes, as Mrs. Heesom claimed, was at the house the day before Sarah died or that she gave the child poison.

After an absence of 30 minutes the jury returned to convict Mrs. Heesom.

"You have been found guilty of a crime of almost unparalleled atrocity," the judge then told the prisoner. "You are a woman devoid of all natural feelings, even to the natural instincts that the brute creation possesses. You have murdered two of your children and you have also murdered your own mother. If it had not been so clearly proven, it would appear incredible that a woman could be so debased, so lost to all natural feeling, as to do what you have done."

He then sentenced her to death.

Mrs. Heesom had shown no emotion on hearing the verdict, but at the conclusion of the judge's speech she threw herself back in her chair, and putting her hands on the front of the dock, rested upon them. But she remained silent.

Mr. Swetenham then asked the judge to instruct a jury of matrons from within the court to ascertain Mrs. Heesom's condition, as she claimed to be pregnant. The doors of the court were closed so that no-one could leave, while a number of suitable women were assembled to find out if Mrs. Heesom was "of child with a quick [living] child." Dr. McEwen, the surgeon at Chester Gaol, was asked to help and advise them.

Half an hour later the jury returned to confirm that Mrs. Heesom was pregnant. She was again placed in the dock and Mr. Justice Lush told her that her execution would be postponed until "a reasonable time after your delivery."

It was thought that this would not be until mid-July. The trial over, Edward Heesom was released from custody.

There had been no irrefutable proof that his partner either procured arsenic or administered it. The evidence against her had been entirely circumstantial, and it was perhaps because of this that she was reprieved on June 23rd, 1878, her sentence being commuted to penal servitude for life.

The press considered her a cold, heartless woman who thought nothing of despatching her nearest and dearest for a quick profit, but there was equally strong criticism of insurance practices.

The agent who had encouraged Mrs. Heesom to increase her policy on her mother was suspended by his employers. Such practices, the *Manchester Evening News* argued, also gave "parents an immediate and considerable money interest in the death of their children."

15
THE COOLEST KILLER

"I am not guilty of this crime"

CHILDREN TELL amazing whoppers, and as gate-keeper at Blackburn's Witton Park, Ellen Ormerod had heard them all over the years. Yet little Harry Ridings seemed genuinely upset.

"Tell me again, lad, what did thee see?" she asked, taking the boy gently by the shoulders. White-faced and shaking, Harry repeated his story. He said that a few minutes earlier, at 12.55, as he was making his way home from school through the park at lunch-time, he had noticed a man lurking in the corner behind the park gates.

Although the man had his back to him, Harry could see that he was carrying a child in his arms.

As the boy watched, the man threw the child down and ran off over the bridge towards Spring Lane. Harry waited to see the little girl get up, but she just lay on her stomach in the wet grass and never stirred.

Terrified, Harry had run straight to Mrs. Ormerod.

Tuesday, November 8th, 1892, was a cold, damp day and she did not want to leave her warm fire, but what if the boy were telling the truth? Wrapping her shawl tightly around her shoulders, Mrs. Ormerod followed Harry back across the park. Then she stopped. There, lying face-down on the ground, was the crumpled body of a little girl, just as Harry had said.

Mrs. Ormerod knelt and touched the child's leg. It was

ice-cold. With her heart pounding, the gate-keeper hurried off to find a policeman.

She soon spotted Police Constable Ashworth, who returned with her to the park. Turning the child's body over, he saw that she had a gash on her forehead, and her clothes were torn. Something red protruded from her mouth, and at first he though it must be her tongue. But it turned out to be a coarse red handkerchief, stuffed with such force into the child's mouth that it had suffocated her.

Near the body Ashworth spotted the clear imprint of a heavily nailed boot. Later, a cast would be taken of it.

The corpse was taken to the local police station, where Dr. Wheatley, the police-surgeon, examined it. He confirmed that the child had been suffocated and found no evidence of sexual assault.

After the post-mortem Edward Barnes identified the victim as his nine-year-old daughter, Polly. He said that on the morning of November 8th she had gone to school, returning as usual at about noon. Shortly before one o'clock he had sent her and her younger sister Mary to Witton Park to graze his cows. Ten minutes later Mary, having run on ahead of Polly, returned home alone. Barnes had been on his way to look for his daughter when he had seen a horrified cluster of people gathered round Polly's body.

On the night of November 13th Superintendent Myers, leading the investigation, sent four constables to see Cross Duckworth, a 32-year-old labourer living in Bower House Fold.

The constables' banging on the front door brought the labourer down in his nightshirt, carrying a candle.

"Are you Cross Duckworth?" he was asked, and he nodded.

"Do you know that we are police officers?"

"Have you come for me about that murder?" Duckworth asked.

Not a word had been spoken about the crime or the purpose of the officers' visit . . . or so they said.

After examining the suspect's boots, they asked if he had a second pair.

He said he did not, but the constables found a second pair on the stairs. They were examined and found to correspond with the cast of the boot-print taken from beside Polly Barnes's body. Questioned about the boots, Duckworth claimed he had not worn them for over a week.

A further search of the house discovered a handkerchief similar in colour and material to the one found in the victim's mouth, and Duckworth was taken to the police station to be questioned by Myers.

Asked about his movements on the morning of November 8th, he claimed he had been drinking and had gone home at one o'clock for his midday meal. There were no witnesses to confirm this — his wife worked and did not come home at that time of day and his two children had eaten and gone back to school before he came home. They later said that when they got home from school they had found that the bowl their father usually ate from had been used.

Checking Duckworth's claim that he had spent most of the morning of the day in question drinking, Myers interviewed Robert Cook, the landlord of the Unicorn Inn in Blackburn. He had known Duckworth for 14 years, and recalled that he had spent the entire morning at the Unicorn, leaving at about 12.40. He had drunk three gills of porter, and when Mrs. Cook invited him to stay and have lunch with them he had declined, saying. "No, I think I will go home."

Both the landlord and his wife said that Duckworth was sober when he left, and Cook saw him again shortly after that evening.

Duckworth had come into the Cooks' kitchen, and read the account of the murder in the evening paper.

Cook said he had not noticed anything strange about the suspect. His voice had never trembled as he read the newspaper report aloud to the company in the kitchen, and nobody observed any sign of guilt.

It was the evidence of others that was to put Cross Duckworth in the dock. Edith Duxbury, a 12-year-old half-timer in the cotton mill at Witton, was coming home from work that afternoon when she saw some cows crossing the brook at the bottom of Spring Lane. Polly and Mary Barnes, whom she knew well, were taking them over the bridge, on which Edith noticed a man standing looking into the water.

Harry Ridings's sister Elizabeth also noticed the man on the bridge. Although neither witness got a close look at him, both later picked out Duckworth at separate identity parades.

Another little girl, Martha Southworth, said she had seen a man run up Spring Lane shortly after 1 o'clock on the day of the murder and had gone to her window to watch him. She too picked out Duckworth at an identity parade.

Mrs. Eliza Woods, landlady of the Turner's Arms, remembered Duckworth coming in on November 8th at 12.40. He drank a small bottle of soda and left. He was not drunk, she said, but another woman, Mary Davies, remembered seeing Duckworth staggering in the street, the worse for drink. She could not recall the time, but another witness, Richard Porter, said he saw Duckworth heading for Witton Park at about 12.50. He was sure of the time because of the gun fired on the hour in Witton Park.

Tried at Liverpool Assizes on December 12th, 1892, for the murder of Polly Barnes, Cross Duckworth heard the evidence of Edith Duxbury and Elizabeth Ridings — who had seen the man only from behind — and Martha Southworth who also identified him.

William Stirrup, a bootmaker, said he had compared the cast of the bootprint with Duckworth's boot, and the two matched.

Duckworth's defence counsel, Mr. McKean, pointed out that such boots were common in Blackburn, but Stirrup insisted that Duckworth's boot and the one which had left the tell-tale impression were one and the same.

Thomas Birtwhistle, inspector of factories and for 32

years secretary to the local Weavers' Association, said he had many years' practical experience as a weaver. He had examined two red handkerchiefs handed to him by Superintendent Myers. They were similar but not identical. There were several technical differences between the handkerchief taken from the mouth of the dead girl and the one found at Duckworth's home.

The defence argued that the handkerchief, like the boot, was a commonplace article, and many had been sold in Blackburn.

In his closing speech for the defence, Mr. McKeand cautioned the jury against putting too much reliance on the testimony of the child witnesses, and claimed that the evidence of the boot and handkerchiefs had been clearly "scattered to the winds."

Mr. Justice Grantham, summing-up, told the jury that the evidence of the boot and handkerchiefs could not be relied upon. But he said that testimony of the children should not be discounted simply because they were young. He said he believed that children, being impressionable, would remember more than an adult.

The jury found Cross Duckworth guilty after an hour's deliberation, and he was sentenced to death.

"I have nothing to say, except what has been said. I am not guilty of the crime," Duckworth told the court.

On Tuesday, January 3rd, 1893, he went to the gallows at Walton Gaol, Liverpool, still protesting his innocence.

One man with serious doubts about the hanged man's guilt was Walter Stirrup, an architect who took an interest in the case. Visiting the home of Martha Southworth, he found that she could not have seen anyone running up Spring Lane from her window.

And although other witnesses said they saw Duckworth in the park that day, this was hardly surprising, as he lived only yards from it.

Consider also his calmness in reading out a report of Polly Barnes's murder. If he were really the killer, he was one of the coolest on record ...

16
TO MAKE AN HONEST WOMAN

She yearned for a life of debauchery

GIVEN AN unexpected half-day holiday from the Failsworth foundry where he worked as a labourer, 20-year-old Levi Taylor decided to spend it a few miles away, whooping it up in Manchester.

It was a warm Saturday in October 1862, and for the first hour he wandered around the bustling shops and busy street markets. Then as evening fell he was drawn to a less respectable part of the city. Shudehill was once where farmers had their horses shod on their way to market, but it had now become a huddle of dilapidated beerhouses and brothels. This was where lonely soldiers garrisoned around the city could spend a week's pay in a single night, and often did.

It was in one of these squalid retreats that Taylor first set eyes on Mary Ann Bradbury. She was knocking back drinks with a soldier who suddenly got rough and started pulling at her dress.

Before he knew it, Taylor was on his feet and defending her. The soldier, slightly the worse for drink, was easy to subdue, and he staggered off. Mary Ann went to sit with her champion, and over drinks she told him her history.

She said she was a country girl, from Bakewell in Derbyshire, and had been sent into domestic service at 14. Finding the work not to her liking, she had run away to Manchester and soon found the life of a prostitute both temperamentally and economically more rewarding than skivvying.

Taylor was taken aback by her forthrightness. She was quite unlike any other girl he knew, and he was fascinated. He took her for a walk in the street market, and when she admired a shawl, he bought it for her. It cost him nearly all he had, but he didn't mind. By now he was infatuated.

Fingering her new shawl, Mary Ann was happy too. She didn't get treats like that every day. All too soon it was time for Levi Taylor to run for his train, but he promised to see her again as soon as he could.

Mary Ann, as she proudly showed off her shawl to the other girls at the pub, probably thought Taylor stupid for parting with so much and asking so little in return. It is doubtful if she gave him another thought, but the following Saturday evening he was back in Shudehill in his Sunday best and carrying a posy of flowers.

He now spent every Saturday evening with Mary Ann, sometimes staying until Sunday morning. At first she was flattered and amused by his devotion, but as the weeks passed she became irritated by the way he monopolised her.

He was jealous if she showed the slightest interest in any other man, for Mary Ann wasn't into fidelity. She was used to playing the field, and realised that Taylor was expecting more in return for that shawl than she had ever imagined. Inevitably, the evening came when her patience snapped and she told him to get lost.

But rejection only intensified his obsession and he grew even more possessive. In desperation, Mary Ann left the pub in Shudehill and went to a brothel in Copperas Street. Levi, however, wasn't to be shaken off that easily. It wasn't long before Mary Ann looked up one evening to see him peering at her through the tobacco-stained window.

Going down on his knees, he told her he loved her. He said he desperately wanted to marry her and take her away from her life of sin. At first Mary Ann sensibly refused him. But then she changed her mind and accepted.

Perhaps she fancied the novelty of becoming a wife. Whatever her reason, she and Taylor were married on December 1st, 1862, at Manchester Cathedral, little more than a stone's throw from Shudehill.

None of Taylor's disapproving family was present. And the ceremony was barely over when Mary Ann, true to form, slipped out through a side door of the cathedral and into a nearby inn to meet a soldier.

When she returned later that afternoon to the ever-forgiving Taylor she was completely drunk. A friend and fellow-prostitute Theresa Sheridan, who liked Levi and disapproved of Mary Ann's treatment of him, was appalled by her friend's behaviour. As she waved the young couple off from Victoria Station on the train to Failsworth, she must have sensed that the marriage was doomed.

Barely a fortnight later Mary Ann had had enough of life as a housewife. She took what money she could find in the rented house in Back Lane, packed a bag and caught the next train back to Manchester. Taylor was distraught when he returned to find her gone. He immediately went after her, finding her in the Copperas Street brothel, where he pleaded with her to come home with him, and she reluctantly agreed. A week later she ran off again, and this time Taylor decided not to follow her. He saw the New Year in alone.

Weeks later, however, in January 1863 one of his colleagues mentioned that he had seen Mary Ann in the Jolly Hatters in Shudehill. Taylor put down his tools, walked out of the foundry and took the train to Manchester.

He went straight to the Jolly Hatters, where he found his wife serving drinks and laughing with customers. There was an ugly scene as he accused Mary Ann of infidelity. She retorted angrily that she was employed as a barmaid, not a prostitute, and Thomas Schofield, the landlord, confirmed this. Levi Taylor did not believe them, but as tempers cooled, Mary Ann agreed to have a drink with him. She refused to return home, however, telling him firmly that she knew what she wanted from life and it wasn't married life in Failsworth.

Taylor wouldn't give up. He moved into lodgings in Manchester and went back to the Jolly Hatters on January 29th and 30th. Each time there was a scene and Schofield threw him out. But Taylor walked in again at 3 p.m. on January 31st, to find Mary Ann, Theresa Sheridan and Schofield having a drink together. Schofield was all for chucking him out, but as Taylor was sober and in a sunny mood, the landlord allowed him to stay.

Looking more cheerful than he had for a long time, Taylor ordered beer for himself and Theresa.

"What!" Mary Ann cried, hands on hips. "Not buying me a drink, your own wife?" Taylor said he thought she'd had enough, but he then bought her one.

When it was served he announced that he had some good news for his wife. He would be leaving on the 4.30 p.m. train to Failsworth and she would never have to see him again.

"I've heard that before," Mary Ann laughed sceptically, but Taylor insisted he meant it and asked her to sing him a farewell song. She obliged, with Theresa at the piano. Then Taylor asked Mary Ann to go upstairs with him to say goodbye in private. A few minutes later, as Theresa sat idly fingering the keys of the piano she heard a sudden screech.

Mary Ann appeared at the top of the stairs. She was clutching her throat and blood poured through her fingers. As she staggered down to the tap-room she opened her mouth, but no words came — only blood. Theresa took her arm and helped her to the sofa.

Then Taylor, his eyes glinting with excitement, appeared at the top of the stairs, his hands dripping blood.

"Fetch a policeman, Theresa. I've killed the bastard!" he said.

At 4 p.m. Police Constable John Bell was patrolling Smithfield Market when he saw people running down Shudehill. Following them into the Jolly Hatters, he saw

Mary Ann lying on the sofa with blood flowing from her neck, forming a pool around her. Near her two men were struggling. One, Constable Bell knew, was the landlord, Thomas Schofield. The other was a young man he didn't recognise, but whose hands were covered in blood.

From the remarks of the people around him, Bell realised that the young man was the injured woman's husband and he had attacked her. There was no time to find out more because a cab arrived to take Mary Ann to the nearby Royal Infirmary.

By now Constable Powers had arrived, and he held Taylor while Bell helped to carry the girl to the cab. She was unconscious by the time she arrived at the hospital, and died within two minutes of being carried inside.

Returning to the Jolly Hatters, Constable Bell joined Constable Powers in questioning Taylor. Grinning insanely, the young labourer kept repeating, "It is well, I have done it. It is well, I have done it." Then he said that he had asked Mary Ann to go upstairs with him to say goodbye. He had persuaded her to lie down on the bed so he could embrace her one last time. Then he'd caught sight of some letters to her from a soldier named Walsh. They had been on the table beside her bed.

Losing his head, he had leaned forward and cut her throat. When that did not kill her, he'd raised her head and slashed her again.

"I had a knife in my pocket," he told the officers, and it transpired that he had bought it earlier that afternoon for a shilling in the Deansgate Market. He had hidden the knife in the privy at the rear of the pub, and he led the constable to it. He had loved Mary Ann dearly, he said, and would not have killed her if she had only behaved properly.

Then his mad grin returned and he began chatting about his own life, referring to the murder flippantly.

His wild look had gone, however, when he appeared before Baron Martin at Liverpool Assizes on Saturday, March 28th, 1863, pleading not guilty to the charge of his wife's murder.

Mr. Owen Jones, a house surgeon at the Royal Infirmary, told the court that Mary Ann Taylor had received two throat wounds from which she had died. One extended from below her left ear and across the centre of her neck, severing her jugular veins and windpipe. The second wound was on the right side, extending from the angle of the jaw to the centre of the neck. Mr. Jones added that if skilled attention had been paid immediately to the wounds, the bleeding might have been stopped, although he could not say whether Mary Ann would have lived.

Thomas Schofield testified that he had just gone down to his cellar when he'd heard a dreadful scream. He'd come rushing back into the tap-room and had seen Mary Ann standing on the stairs, covered in blood. A moment later, Taylor appeared behind her and announced that he had killed her.

Schofield said he had run to him and demanded the knife, but Taylor insisted he didn't have one. Then he'd looked down at his bloody hands and asked if he could go out into the yard to wash them. Schofield had allowed him to do so, watching from the door, but when Taylor returned a few moments later, his hands still bloody, the landlord suspected that he had gone into the yard to hide the knife.

Cross-examined by Mr. Ernest Jones, defending, Schofield said that the Jolly Hatter was only a registered lodging house.

"Is it not also a brothel?" the defence counsel asked.

Schofield looked down and after a moment admitted that it was.

"And don't you engage the girls in your employ for the purposes of the brothel?"

"Yes sir, I do," Schofield replied in little more than a whisper.

"Did you engage Mary Ann Taylor as a prostitute?"

"No sir," Schofield answered firmly. "She was merely a servant in the house."

Theresa Sheridan told the court that in her opinion

Taylor had been fond of Mary Ann, perhaps too fond. He was always trying to get her away from evil influences and bad companions, and Theresa said she had felt truly sorry for him.

William Quinn, the owner of the inn where Taylor had taken lodgings, remembered him coming in on the night of January 30th. After getting thoroughly drunk, Taylor had said that if he could not have his wife, no one would. "I will take her life even if I swing for it," he had declared.

Constable Powers testified that Taylor had rambled on so excitedly in making his confession, that he seemed insane. The officer added that he had been so worried about Taylor's state of mind that after arresting him he had sat up with him all night in his cell at Street police station.

Several witnesses travelled from Failsworth to Liverpool to testify to Taylor's good characer. His employer, John Day, said Taylor had been a good worker until his marriage, after which he had downed tools from time to go in search of his wife. He had finally walked out on January 28th.

Jonah Dobson, an inspector of Sunday schools, said that Taylor had regularly attended Sunday school for nine months prior to the murder, and for the last two months, during his marriage, he had been a teacher.

In his concluding speech for the defence Mr. Jones said that Taylor had married a common prostitute, hoping to make an honest woman of her. He had taken her back to Failsworth in the hope they might have a proper married life, but Mary Ann so yearned for the life of debauchery that she ran away from her husband not once, but twice.

The defence counsel claimed that when Taylor asked her to say goodbye in private, that was all he intended to do. But when he had seen the love letters to her from another man, he had been driven mad, taken a knife he happened to have in his pocket, and killed her.

Mr. Jones argued that Taylor was guilty only of manslaughter because the extreme provocation by his wife had brought on temporary insanity. The counsel's speech was so moving that when he had finished many in court were in tears. Taylor himself broke down whenever Mary Ann's name was mentioned.

But in his summing-up the judge said, "It is a melancholy thing to see a young man who has received such a good character placed in such a position, but the facts are clear and unalterable. The prisoner could be guilty of manslaughter, but his act was premeditated as he had bought a knife that same afternoon. He had also been heard to threaten his wife's life the previous evening at his lodgings."

The plea of insanity was also, in the judge's opinion, very dubious, and the jury convicted Taylor of murder, but with a recommendation for mercy.

"You have been found guilty on evidence which it is impossible for any jury to resist, however strongly they may feel for you," the judge then told the prisoner, sentencing him to death.

In a state of collapse, Levi Taylor had to be supported by two officers who carried him from the dock. But the jury's recommendation did not go unheeded. On Monday, April 6th, 1863, Taylor's sentence was commuted to penal servitude for life.

22
"HARTLEY, THE RIBCHESTER MURDERER"

Cries of "Lynch 'em! Lynch 'em!" came from the crowd

" **S**HE LAY sprawled upon the bed naked from the waist down, her head and face were covered in blood which still oozed and dripped. Her hands had been fastened roughly by the wrists to the bedposts, while a piece of ragged shawl was tied tightly around her throat ..."

In stunned silence the inquest jury at the White Bull Inn, in the Lancashire village of Ribchester, heard Police Sergeant Whiteside describe what met his eyes when he entered the bedroom of Mrs. Ann Walne, a 79-year-old widow.

He had been summoned to the house by Joseph Ward, who Mrs. Walne employed to feed her cattle. Ward had arrived at her home on Fleet Street Lane, half-way between Ribchester and Longridge, at 6 o'clock on the morning of Tuesday, November 11th, 1862. Unusually, Mrs. Walne, an early riser, was not up and about. When Ward got no response no matter how hard he knocked, he went round to the back door. Finding a downstairs window had been forced, he hurried off to seek Sergeant Whiteside.

The policeman was sure the murderer's motive was robbery. Mrs. Walne, remarkably active for her age, ran a beerhouse from her home, known locally as the "Joiners'

Arms." She also had a smallholding on which she kept four cows. All this had inspired rumours that she was a miser, keeping large sums of money hidden in her bed.

Her son John confirmed that his mother, who lived alone, did indeed hide money in this way. His wife, while making the bed, had often found coins concealed there. As no money had been found either in or near the bed, Whiteside assumed it had been taken by Mrs. Walne's murderer or murderers — boot-prints leading through the snow from the broken back window to the lane suggested that there had been more than one intruder.

Dr. Maitland, who had carried out a post-mortem examination, told the coroner that Mrs. Walne had been beaten so savagely about the head and face that her nose, temple-bone and upper jaw were all broken. But this was not what had killed her. He believed she had first been knocked unconcious and then suffocated, either with her pillow or with the bedsheets.

Despite her nakedness she had not been sexually assaulted. He could not be certain how long she had been dead, but the police knew she was still alive at 8 o'clock the previous evening. She was standing at her door when Joseph Ward passed on his way home. As it was snowing heavily, she had asked him to help her close her shutters. When he had done so she wished him "Good night," and he heard her bolt her door from the inside.

The inquest jury returned a verdict of wilful murder against some person or persons unknown, and the coroner announced a government reward of £100 for information leading to the arrest of the killers.

Meanwhile the villagers of Ribchester, many of whom had known Mrs. Walne all their lives as "Old Nanny," trudged in pilgrimage down the lane to her lonely cottage and stood in silent vigil outside.

The police, led by Superintendent McNab, began their search for the killers at Ribchester Workhouse, which accommodated many criminals. One was Tom Davis, elderly and vicious-looking. On the day prior to the murder he had visited Mrs. Walne, seeking work for the winter.

Jim Whalley, busy whitewashing the house, had been struck by Davis's strange manner and the furtive way he looked around Mrs. Walne's front-room. On hearing of the murder Whalley had gone straight to the police.

Apparently Mrs. Walne hadn't liked the look of Davis either, for she had sent him packing. Hugh Harrison, another workhouse resident, told McNab that Mrs. Walne was Davis's favourite topic of conversation. "The old woman will have money planted somewhere," he would often say, "either in the cloakcase or some unlikely place ... I'll make her so that she can't speak." Davis had also told Harrison: "Thous may as weel go with us, and make a man i'th' job."

Harrison had asked him where he meant to go. When he replied, "To old Ann Walne's," Harrison claimed he had refused, adding that he had "suffered enough and would suffer no more for anybody."

Confronted by McNab, Davis said that Harrison had told nothing but lies. The superintendent nevertheless arrested him, together with Charles Fishwick and Stephen Balshaw, two other workhouse inmates, and all three were taken to Preston's House of Correction. But the sad truth was that the inquiry was getting nowhere.

Then nine days after the murder, at 10 p.m. on November 20th, Tom Bowling, gamekeeper and local villain, also known as "Chorley Tom," called on a former cell-mate, Duncan McPhail, at his home near Belle Vue Gardens in Blackburn, 10 miles from Ribchester.

Bowling hoped his friend would help him move house. McPhail, 34, the son of a preacher, was a petty crook who also went from town to town with his horse and cart, selling cheese and bacon. As the two chatted Bowling mentioned the recent murder at Ribchester. "I hear," he said, "they've been trying those men again for the murder of the old woman. Dost think they will be guilty?"

"They're none guilty," McPhail laughed. "I'll tell thee

who did it if you promise not to tell." Bowling promised. "There were me, Dan Carr, Bill Woods, George Woods and Ben Hartley."

"How much money did you get?" asked Bowling, astonished.

"Not much," McPhail sighed.

Bowling wondered why they'd killed Mrs. Walne. "Could not you do it without," he asked, "seeing there was only one woman in the house? Why did you murder her?"

"Because the old devil wouldn't tell where her money was."

Suddenly McPhail's wife appeared on the stairs. "Hush, folks will hear ye outside," she warned.

Her husband told her to shut up and go back to bed. At the door Bowling demanded a share of the plunder. McPhail told him this was impossible as they had now spent the money.

"Oh, I'll take anything else you got then — clothes, pots, whatever," said Bowling. But McPhail insisted they had taken only money.

Annoyed, Bowling wondered how he might use his newly acquired knowledge. He knew of the £100 reward offered for information leading to the killers' capture, but he also knew the fate of squealers. Nevertheless, a few days later he went to see Superintendent McNab, telling him of his conversation with McPhail.

It was not because of the reward alone that he had come forward, he insisted. He was concerned about the fate of the three men held in Preston's House of Correction. "It is not right the innocent should suffer," he told McNab.

On November 30th the superintendent arrested Duncan McPhail; George Woods, 45; his brother William, 33; Dan Carr, 34; and Ben Hartley, 53, and charged them all with the murder. He already knew McPhail and Carr to be criminals and that Carr had served time for manslaughter. But he knew nothing of George and William Woods or Ben Hartley.

On December 2nd all five appeared before the magistrates at Blackburn Police Court, where Tom Bowling recounted his conversation with McPhail on the evening of November 20th. McPhail, leaning forward, angrily accused him of lying and claimed he had never seen him on the night in question.

The five suspects were remanded in custody, and after they had been taken back to their cells in the police station a subdued Ben Hartley asked to see Superintendent McNab. In a quiet voice he told the policeman that the murder had weighed heavily on his conscience, and he now wished to make a confession.

Unlike McPhail and Carr, Hartley was not a criminal but earned a living as a power-loom weaver. He told McNab he had known Dan Carr for 15 years and George Woods since he was discharged from the army the previous May. He had first met McPhail at the Preston Guild festivities in September, when they had been introduced by a mutual friend, Tom Bowling.

A few days before the murder Hartley had visited McPhail, who told him that while hawking cheese and bacon at Ribchester he had popped into Mrs. Walne's beerhouse. According to a conversation he had overheard, she had recently sold a cow and hidden the money in her bed.

"We must have it," he said. He and Hartley, together with George Woods and Dan Carr, with whom he had already discussed the matter, must go to Mrs. Walne's home and take the money. At first, Hartley said, he told McPhail that he cared "nowt about it" and didn't want to be involved. But McPhail persuaded him.

The following Friday evening at 6 o'clock, McPhail, Woods, Carr and Hartley met as arranged at Salford Bridge, Blackburn. But they couldn't go to Mrs. Walne's house that night because it was a full moon. They therefore agreed to meet on Sunday night, but George Woods turned up drunk and the venture again had to be postponed, much to McPhail's annoyance.

The following evening they all met again on Salford Bridge, and although it was snowing they all decided to set off for Ribchester.

Hartley said he didn't take a weapon, but Dan Carr was armed with a cane walking-stick tipped with lead, as was Woods, who also carried a crowbar. McPhail had a lantern and a pistol. Huddled under umbrellas, they went up Penney Street, past the Bull's Head and then down Parker's Brow. At Ribchester the church clock was striking eight when they crossed the bridge.

As it was still snowing, Woods suggested they shelter in a nearby cow-shed, but McPhail wouldn't hear of it. "There's a footpath up to the old woman's," he said, "let us take it — it'll be the quietest there."

They then cut across fields until they came to a barn which Woods forced open with his crowbar, and here they sheltered until well after midnight. McPhail and Carr each had a bottle of rum which they passed around. Then McPhail said, "Come on, it's time to begin. Let's go." Mrs. Walne's house was nearby. As both doors were bolted and the windows shuttered and barred, Carr removed an entire downstairs window.

Once inside the house Carr lit the lantern and they went upstairs. When they entered Mrs. Walne's bedroom they found her sitting up in bed, her eyes wide with terror.

"Where's thy money?" Woods demanded. She made no reply, but began to scream. As she tried to get out of bed Hartley pushed her back and held her while Woods searched the mattress for the money.

Finding it, they went back downstairs and began ransacking the cupboards and drawers in case there was more. Meanwhile Mrs. Walne was still screaming, so Carr dashed upstairs, brandishing his lead-tipped walking-stick.

"I'll stop her making that din!" he shouted as the others followed. Strong despite her age, Mrs. Walne struggled so hard that Hartley said he had to hold her head so that Carr could hit her with the cane. He thought Carr meant only to stun her, he insisted. But Carr missed and struck him on the hand instead, causing him to cry out. "Did I hit thee?" Carr grunted.

"Aye," said Hartley, rubbing his swollen hand, which McNab saw was bruised. Carr then struck the old woman twice on the side of the head, "which made her head rattle," Hartley told the superintendent.

"Oh, dear!" Mrs. Walne cried. "You have killed me!" But Carr said she was probably only unconscious, and he suggested they tie her up in case she raised the alarm before they could get away.

Woods ran back downstairs, found two handkerchiefs and tied her wrists to the bedposts. Hartley was certain she was still alive when they left the room because he could hear her moaning. He did not recall a piece of shawl being tied around Mrs. Walne's neck, or any attempt to smother her. The four intruders then left the house and took the road through Longridge towards Preston.

On the Preston Road they divided the spoils. Woods, who had found Mrs. Walne's money under her mattress wrapped up in a piece of old flannel, at first said they had got £40. But when he examined the money he realised that silver coins were mixed with the gold sovereigns, which meant there was in fact only £18 2s. Each man got four gold sovereigns (worth £1 each) and 10s 6d in silver.

After throwing away their weapons — Hartley saw Carr take the lead off his cane before flinging the stick away — they split up. McPhail and Woods went to Bamber Bridge near Preston, where they caught a train to Blackburn. Hartley and Carr walked on to Preston. Arriving there at 5.15 a.m., they stopped for a drink at an inn near the House of Correction. They each had two glasses of whisky, paying for them with the dead woman's silver. At 6 a.m. — 12 hours after setting out for Ribchester — they went to the station and caught the first train to Blackburn.

The next day Hartley called on Dan Carr, who told him that McPhail, George Woods and his brother William had hired a cab and gone off on a drinking spree.

Hartley told McNab that he and Carr also drank most of

their share of the money. With tears streaming down his cheeks, he insisted he had never meant to harm Mrs. Walne. As Hartley was not the one who had actually killed her, and the police were eager to convict the man who had, he was allowed to turn "approver," giving Queen's Evidence. Although his confession had implicated McPhail, George Woods and Carr, it exonerated William Woods, who was immediately released from custody.

Committed for trial, the four men were ordered to be taken to Liverpool's Kirkdale Prison. As news of their imminent departure spread through Blackburn on December 10th excited crowds began to gather near the Town Hall, where the police station was situated. When the four were brought out they were greeted with boos and jeers, and then with cries of "Lynch 'em! Lynch 'em!" As the crowd surged towards them the police struggled to protect the prisoners.

While Woods, McPhail and Carr travelled in one van, Hartley rode separately in another with Superintendent Higgs. Once they were all safely inside the vans, the horses were whipped-up and galloped to Blackburn Station, pursued by the mob all the way to the station platform.

On March 30th, 1863, Duncan McPhail and George Woods pleaded not guilty when they appeared at Liverpool Assizes before Baron Martin.

Dan Carr was to have stood beside them, but was conspicuous by his absence and beyond the reach of the law. Described as a "short man, badly pock-marked and of forbidding appearance," he had told warders he lived in terror of being hanged. He denied murdering Mrs. Walne, claiming that though he had struck her twice with his stick, these were light blows meant only to stun her. One of the others, he claimed, had suffocated her while she lay unconscious.

His horror of the gallows was so great that ever since his arrival at Kirkdale he had suffered from bouts of asthma. On the morning of the trial he had been shaved and appeared quite well. Then at 7 o'clock he had sat down on a chair, thrown back his head and died of a heart attack!

The case against McPhail and Woods rested almost wholly on the confession of Ben Hartley, who said he had turned informer out of guilt. Reporters covering the trial, however, commented that he was merely out to save his own neck, and the only way he could do that was by putting the rope firmly around the necks of his two "friends."

After Hartley had described the events leading up to the murder, witnesses were called to confirm various parts of his story.

Hartley had testified that when the four men left Blackburn for Ribchester they had encountered a man on Parker's Brow, exchanging a few comments with him about the appalling weather. Robert Jackson, a farmer, remembered meeting four men at Parker's Brow in Blackburn in the early evening of November 10th. They'd carried umbrellas, and one of the men — he believed it was Hartley — had remarked, "It's a stormy night." Jackson had agreed it was "roguish."

Joseph Molyneux, a weaver from Ribchester, was walking to Preston at 2.50 on the morning of November 11th when he noticed the footprints of four men in the snow. The prints had not been made by clogs, but boots. The four suspects had all worn boots that night.

William Massey, head porter at Preston Station, identified Hartley and Carr as two men who had boarded the first train out on November 11th.

Superintendent McNab then described what he had found on arriving at Mrs. Walne's home after the murder. Both the upper and lower rooms had been ransacked, and the clock, the case of which had been damaged during the search for the old lady's money, had stopped at 2.17 — about the time Hartley said he and the other men had entered the house.

In the snow near the broken back window the superintendent had seen the impressions of four sets of boots. Similar boot-prints were outside a nearby barn which showed signs of having been broken into. Casts had been taken of these prints, which had subsequently been found to match the boots worn by the four suspects.

Searching the area where Hartley said the others had discarded their weapons, the police had found a crowbar, bits of broken walking-sticks and a piece of old flannel which was identified as having belonged to Mrs. Walne.

Despite this evidence the defence argued that much of Hartley's testimony was uncorroborated. But after an hour's absence the jury returned with verdicts of "Guilty," though with a recommendation to mercy. Both men were then sentenced to death.

The following day Ben Hartley appeared before the court, charged with Mrs. Walne's murder and pleading not guilty. In exchange for his testimony the previous day the prosecution offered no evidence, and he was discharged.

In Blackburn feeling ran high, many believing there had been a miscarriage of justice. Petitions for McPhail and Woods were signed and sent to the Home Secretary, Sir George Grey, urging clemency on the grounds that neither man had taken part in the actual murder, while the two who had — Hartley and Carr — had escaped punishment. But the Home Secretary refused to intervene.

It was noted that the petition for Woods had attracted more signatures than that for McPhail. But whereas McPhail was a petty criminal, Woods was regarded as a decent man who had served 12 honourable years in the army, fighting with valour in both India and the Crimea. But on his discharge from the army he had found work hard to get and had taken to poaching, falling into bad company.

While awaiting execution McPhail claimed he had been outside the house acting as a "look-out" when the murder took place, and had been opposed to harming Mrs. Walne. Woods also denied involvement in the murder, although he admitted tying the victim's hands to her bedposts and being in the room when she was struck.

At noon on Saturday, April 25th, 1863, Duncan McPhail and George Woods were publicly hanged outside Kirkdale Prison. When they walked out together Woods, though pale, seemed calm and composed. McPhail, however, was visibly distressed and trembling. Just before the trap-door bolt was drawn, the executioner William Calcraft followed his custom of shaking hands with the condemned men, pressing McPhail's several times.

Meanwhile expressions of sympathy came from the 50,000-strong crowd, which included many spectators from Blackburn.

The bolt was then drawn, Woods dying instantly, but McPhail struggling convulsively for several seconds.

Did Hartley, described by one contemporary newspaper as "the main villain in this foul drama of murder," escape justice? Not entirely. On his return to Blackburn after the trial he found a ranting mob awaiting him. Outraged that he had avoided the gallows by betraying his accomplices, they had daubed the front of his house in Pearson Street with the words "Hartley, the Ribchester Murderer."

Fearing for his life, Ben Hartley fled with his family to Preston, never to be seen in Blackburn again.

18
THE GIRL IN THE NEW GREEN HAT

"It's up there, I've done it. It was in the wife's bedroom"

SARAH Clutton loved hats. On the morning of Monday, May 4th, 1925, she went into Lewis's department store in the centre of Manchester and treated herself to a pretty green one she'd had her eye on for some time. It was expensive, but Sarah felt she needed something nice to cheer her up.

The 24-year-old prostitute feared she was "sick" again. Venereal diseases were her occupational hazard, but with a new hat on her head and the warm spring sunshine on her face, she felt much better. All she needed to complete her happiness, she thought, was a drink. But her purchase had left her short of cash, so she'd have to find a man.

As she sauntered down Market Street she saw a likely young chap idly looking in a shop window. "Hullo, lovey," she purred, slipping her hand through his arm. "Are you going to buy me a drink?"

Jim Makin was a 25-year-old bleacher. He had recently married, but he didn't allow this to cramp his style. He continued to drink as heavily as before and to see other women. He had taken a day off work, and had caught a tram into Manchester to meet some pals for a drink. Sarah, however, was a more attractive proposition, so he abandoned his plans and took her to the nearest pub. One beer soon became nine in the three hours they spent touring the city centre bars. Then at 3 o'clock Sarah demanded to be taken to his home.

He tried to explain that this was impossible as his wife would soon be back from work, but Sarah wouldn't take no for an answer. Reluctantly, he boarded the tram with her in Stevenson Square which would take them the four miles to Newton Heath and 3 Cross Street, where he and his young wife Annie had lodged with his uncle, Joe Howsley, since their marriage on January 10th.

Apprehensive in case Annie or his uncle had returned early from work, Makin left Sarah at the top of the street and went alone to the terraced house. A moment later, having made sure the place was empty, he returned to the front door. This was the "all clear" signal to Sarah.

But Makin's actions had not gone unnoticed. Directly opposite the house was Mrs. Hilda Collinge's sweet shop. Inside, she and her assistant Mrs. Gertrude Jackson had seen Makin enter the house and then reappear and stand on the doorstep. Then they saw a young woman in a smart green hat approach down the street. She stopped outside Makin's door, and after a moment's hesitation followed him inside.

The two women observers realised that something "funny" was going on. An hour later they saw Makin leave the house and hurry down the street and onto Oldham Road, where he boarded a tram. They looked back expectantly at the house. But the woman in the green hat did not come out.

At 5.30 p.m. Annie Makin and Joe Howsley arrived home. Annie knew her husband was off work that day and expected him to be awaiting them. She called his name several times, but there was no reply. While Joe went through into the kitchen to put the kettle on for tea, Annie ran up to the bedroom, thinking Jim might be lying down.

But on half opening the door she was startled to see a woman's legs protruding from beneath the bed. Opening the door wider, she saw a pool of blood. She screamed and continued screaming until Joe came up and took her downstairs. Then he ran to Oldham Road and waylaid PC Edward Smith, who returned with him to the house.

Having ascertained that the woman was dead, Smith alerted Newton Heath Police Station, and Superintendent Lansberry arrived, accompanied by Dr. Buck, the police surgeon.

Examining the dead woman, who was almost naked, Buck found that her head had been battered and she had two knife-wounds to her throat. One of them had severed her jugular vein, causing her to bleed to death. A sharp carving knife covered in blood lay near her body.

"Who is she?" the superintendent asked Mr. Howsley.

To his surprise, Uncle Joe said he'd never seen her before.

Fragments of glass littered the bedroom floor, and a man's shirt with blood on the collar and both sleeves lay on the bed. Inspecting it, Lansberry asked who else lived in the house. Joe said his nephew did, and he was missing.

The police immediately issued a description of Makin and a hunt began for him.

At 8.05 that evening Arthur Green was coming out of the Falstaff Hotel in the centre of Manchester when he bumped into his old pal Jim Makin, who was drunk. As they chatted Makin suddenly blurted out that he was under arrest. Laughing, Green told him not to talk nonsense and asked him what he'd done.

"I've done a woman in," Makin told him.

Green, thinking it was just the drink talking, told him to go home.

"I can't go home," said Makin. "It's up there, I've done it. It was in the wife's bedroom."

Shocked, Green asked him if it was "the missis" he had murdered, but Makin shook his head.

"No," he said. "It's one from down town ... it was in the wife's bedroom, and the woman asked for a bowl of water. She then started crying. I hit her on the head with a bottle. I went downstairs, got a knife and drew it across her."

Taking Green's hand and shaking it warmly, he continued: "You're the only pal I have down here tonight, Arthur."

Then he gave Green nine one-pound notes and asked him to take them to Annie, saying that he wouldn't be going home again as he now intended to give himself up to the police.

Meanwhile Superintendent Lansberry had found a letter in the dead woman's handbag, and this had provided him with an address: 13 Manor Street, Ardwick. Going there he discovered it was a women's hostel. One of the residents, Amelia Hughes, accompanied him to the police mortuary where she identified the dead woman as her friend Sadie Clutton.

She said that the previous day Sadie had tearfully told her that she feared she might have a venereal disease.

Lansberry checked the police files and discovered that Sarah Elizabeth Clutton, originally from Liverpool, had several convictions for prostitution under her own name and also various aliases, including May Smith and Mary Barker.

At 9.45 p.m. the superintendent arrived back at Newton Heath Police Station. As he was about to go inside he saw a man stagger off a tram which had stopped nearby. As Lansberry stood and watched, the man came slowly up to him and announced in a slurred voice: "I'm Jim Makin."

He was so drunk that the superintendent had to call two constables to help him into the station, and for the next few hours Makin was left in a cell to sober up. Then he was examined by Dr. Buck who found congealed blood under his fingernails, two recent cuts on his right hand and what appeared to be bloodstains on his trousers.

Charged with Sarah Clutton's murder, Makin replied: "I was under the influence of drink. I thought she had a bad disorder or was in a bad way."

At the inquest on May 5th, presided over by C. W. W. Surridge, Dr. Buck testified that Sarah Clutton had been severely beaten about the head with a beer bottle.

However, what had killed her were two knife wounds to her throat, one of which had caused her to bleed so much that all her internal organs were entirely drained of blood.

The police surgeon said that Sarah had been completely free from disease. She had not had VD or anything else.

After a short retirement the jury brought in a verdict of wilful murder against Makin, who was then taken to Strangeways Prison.

Pleading not guilty when his trial began at Manchester Assizes on Saturday, July 25th, 1925, he told the court that when he and Sarah arrived at his home they had gone straight upstairs to his bedroom, undressed and had sex. Afterwards, Sarah asked him for a bowl of water and then began to cry. Suspecting that she might have a venereal disease, he began questioning her.

When she wouldn't say if she were infected he became angry and told her to put on her clothes and get out, but she said she needed another drink and went towards a bottle of beer standing in a corner of the room.

Instead of putting it to her lips, she rushed at him with it, so he snatched it from her and smashed it against her head. Then he told her to hurry up and get dressed.

As he ran downstairs she screamed in pain and yelled after him, "Come up here again and I will do you the same as you have done to me!"

"I then got hold of a knife," Makin testified, "and went upstairs thinking to frighten her. When I went into the room she rushed me."

He said that in the ensuing struggle they fell to the floor. When they got up he was appalled to see blood on his shirt and blood coming from Sarah's throat. He was too drunk to remember much more.

But Mr. Cyril Atkinson KC, MP, prosecuting, told the court that Makin had been sober enough to have the presence of mind to change his blood-soaked shirt and wipe his bloody hands on a kitchen towel before fleeing the house.

Tom Crawford, the conductor of the tram which Sarah

Clutton and Jim Makin had taken from Stevenson Square to Newton Heath, told the court that he remembered Miss Clutton not only for the distinctive green hat she was wearing, and which he now identified in court, but also because she had smiled at him. He said that although the couple appeared to have been drinking, neither was drunk.

Mr. Gorman, defending, told the court that Makin was an orphan and had suffered from serious mental problems since returning from the war in 1918. He had made three attempts to commit suicide by throwing himself into the Rochdale Canal, but had been rescued on each occasion just as he was about to go under for the last time.

There was also evidence that mental instability ran in the family — Makin's elder brother Frederick had recently died in Prestwich Asylum.

Makin's step-sister, with whom he had lived prior to his marriage, told the court that she had turned him out after he had threatened to kill both her and her husband. She recalled that he had often suffered from bad headaches and was at times "very queer."

Makin's wife testified that since their marriage her husband had often threatened to cut her throat. She had become so alarmed by his mood swings that she had taken to hiding his razor.

But Joe Howsley told a different story. He said that in the few months the couple had lived with him he had never seen Jim drunk or heard him threaten Annie. They seemed to be very happy.

The uncle also said that he had never heard anything about his nephew having mental problems. Under cross-examination, however, he agreed that he had been out of touch with his family for some years prior to his nephew coming to lodge with him.

In his concluding speech the defence counsel argued that Makin was mentally ill at the time of the killing and this condition, together with the heavy drinking he had done that day, meant that he was not responsible for his actions.

But it took the jury only 20 minutes to decide that Jim Makin was guilty of murder, and Mr. Justice Wright then sentenced him to death.

Several women in court burst into tears, but Makin appeared unmoved. He apparently accepted the justice of his sentence, for he subsequently made no appeal.

At 8 a.m. on Tuesday, August 11th, 1925, he was hanged at Strangeways Prison. It was reported that 250 people loitered outside the prison gates, many on their way to work, and when the notice of execution was displayed there was a "morbid rush" to read it.

Was Jim Makin mad? The authorities didn't think so. They later revealed that his behaviour in prison had been exemplary. He had shown no sign of violence whatever.

19
NO IDLE THREAT

"He says he's going to do for thee before Christmas"

SEVENTEEN-YEAR-OLD Kate Garrity first met Jack Griffiths in Shaw, near Oldham, Lancashire, in 1905, when she moved into a house a few doors away from his in Middleton Street. At first she was very attracted to the 19-year-old ex-soldier and they became sweethearts. But Jack was always scrapping with someone, usually over nothing very much, his hot-headedness was more in fun than violent. Eventually, though, his possessiveness and jealousy proved too much for the young lass, so that after one of their frequent quarrels, she told him she didn't want to go out with him again.

Characteristically, Griffiths couldn't accept a decision like that, and pestered her. When she finished work at the mill he would be waiting and follow her all the way to her front door. It annoyed Kate, but didn't cause any real trouble until the day she stopped in the street to speak to her best friend's boy friend, Will Newall. As they chatted Griffiths suddenly came out of nowhere and thrashed the young man to the ground. Will, more lightly built than Jack, was in no mood for a fight, so he scrambled to his feet and ran off as fast as he could go. On another occasion, Kate stopped in the street to chat with a neighbour, a Mrs. Smith, and Griffiths bore down on them, demanding that Kate come for a walk with him. When she refused, he lunged at her, grabbed her arm and dragged the protesting girl after him. As she struggled to get away, he lost his temper completely and punched her hard in the face. Mrs. Smith, outraged by this disgraceful display, tried to intervene, whereupon Griffiths, with clenched fist, threatened to punch her, too. Luckily, a policeman arrived at that moment and Griffiths was arrested.

At the police station he vigorously and vehemently denied having done any real harm to Kate, describing his vicious assault as nothing more than a "love tap." However, when the police saw the girl's bloodied mouth they simply couldn't believe his version of events and Griffiths was bound over to keep the peace for three months.

From then on Jack kept away from Kate. But he still sent a young friend, 14-year-old John Bardsley, to carry messages to his former sweetheart.

Whenever she saw John, Kate's heart sank, for he always seemed to be hanging around with a message for her. Coming out of the corner shop one cold December morning Kate found him standing outside, waiting for her. "Kate! Kate Garrity!" he called. Kate was determined to ignore him and walked on. However, Griffiths had promised the lad sixpence to deliver his message, so deliver the message he would.

"Jack says he wants thee to meet him down by the back of Dawn Mill," said the lad as he caught up with her.

"I'll meet him nowhere!" shouted Kate.

"But he says thee's got to, or else ..." John Bardsley hesitated. "Or else what?" demanded Kate, so angry now that despite the cold she let her shawl slip from her head. Bardsley looked a little uneasy, then grinning awkwardly replied quickly, "Or else, or else he says he's going to do for thee before Christmas."

Christmas! That was only 11 days away. Hopefully, Jack Griffiths was nothing but talk.

On the morning of December 20th, Robert Garrity, who hadn't slept a wink all night, was worried. His daughter,

Kate, had gone out the previous evening at ten past eight to fetch beer from the Blue Bell and hadn't come back. Knowing about the threats Jack Griffiths had been making, Garrity felt certain something dreadful had happened to her. Time and again he had gone up and down the street following her usual route to the pub and back, but, look where he might, could not find her. As soon as dawn came, he put on his coat again, and went back outside. He stopped people on their way to the mill asking if they had seen his Kate, but although most of them knew her very well, none of them had.

But as he was crossing some waste ground close to Greenfield Mill, Mr. Garrity suddenly spotted the beer Kate had taken with her. He picked it up, feeling certain that at last he was close to finding his little girl. There were some sacks piled up against a factory wall close by, and almost without thinking, he went across and lifted one up and saw his daughter's face, stark and lifeless.

Dr. Forbes Kinnear did an immediate post-mortem examination of the dead girl and found numerous marks, but the main cause of her death had been strangulation; a piece of cord or string had been pulled tight around her neck.

Inspector Hyde, who was leading the investigation, observed that there were clog-prints near the body. He traced the prints as far as the Temperance Hall, and as Jack Griffiths was already the prime suspect, asked about him there.

Will Ward and Fred Sutcliffe said that they had seen Jack come into the Temperance Hall at about 9.20 the previous evening. He had washed his hands and gone straight into the billiard room.

Hyde was already aware that two women, Mrs. Morris and Mrs. Leech, had seen Griffiths with a girl at around 8.30, but they hadn't known who she was because of the thick shawl she wore over her head.

Mark Sanders, another witness, said he had seen a couple arguing at the corner of Moss Hey Street and

Greenfield Lane at about 8.45. His attention had been held as he saw the man grasp the woman's shoulder, and heard her cry out in protest. They had walked purposefully off in the direction in which Kate's body was later found.

On being questioned at his home, Griffiths at first denied his meeting with Kate, but when told about the three witnesses he said he'd bumped into her on his way to the Temperance Hall. According to his account, they had exchanged a few words, then parted on friendly terms. He had gone on cheerfully to the Hall, although he could not adequately explain why it had taken him nearly an hour to get there.

Griffiths was taken to Shaw police station for further questioning, and there his clogs were examined to see if they fitted the prints found near the body. They were crucially similar. Not only was the metal stud on the right clog broken just as in the prints, but adhering to the stud were traces of ultramarine, some of which had been found on the prints.

Examining his clothes, police discovered bloodstains on both his shirt and the cuffs of his coat.

He also had in his pocket a small bundle of love letters sent by the dead girl, plus a photograph of her and a wire brooch forming the name Kate. The police also found a long piece of string! Could it have been the murder weapon? They were certain that it was.

Griffiths was arrested and formally charged with the murder of Kate Garrity. His trial began on February 6th, 1906, at Manchester Assizes, before Mr. Justice Grantham. Griffiths maintained his innocence and pleaded not guilty.

Catherine Garrity, Kate's mother, in a state of near-collapse, told the court that her daughter had been bright, lively and healthy, and that she had left the house on the night of her murder perfectly happy. She went on to tell about an extraordinary letter she had received that day from someone in Ashford, Kent. The letter-writer, bearing the initials S.H.B., expressed regret that his "old pal, Jack

Griffiths" was being charged with a crime of which he was innocent. The writer claimed that it was he who had committed the murder after quarrelling with the girl.

William Turner, a man who worked with Griffiths at Lyon Mill, told the court that when he asked Griffiths about Kate on the morning after the murder, he had slumped over a machine and sobbed.

"He said that he'd better go home but I advised him against it as everyone would be staring at him and following him about."

Young John Bardsley told the court about the many messages he had been paid to deliver to Kate from Griffiths and particularly about the one threatening to "do for her before Christmas."

Deborah Blackley, who'd worked alongside Kate at the mill, said she well remembered Griffiths hanging around the workplace a few days before Kate's murder, and hearing him threaten Kate that he would "do for her."

Although the evidence was only circumstantial, it was enough to convince the jury, who took only five minutes to find Griffiths guilty of murder. As the death sentence was passed, he stoically remarked, "I have but once to die." He betrayed no emotion before being led away.

A campaign for Griffiths's reprieve was started immediately by J. H. Butterworth, the Manchester solicitor who represented the defence. Butterworth made much of the anonymous letter from Suffered, Kent, to Kate's mother, particularly the passage which read: "I did not know what to do with the body so I covered it up with sacks."

Butterworth inferred that the murderer probably intended to hide the body in Nalls' Factory, the building adjoining the place where Kate's body had been found. He claimed that the murderer had probably tried to force open the door, but had been unable to do so owing to a big bar behind it. Instead, therefore, he had covered the corpse with sacks. Butterworth also thought, quite rightly, that the strange letter raised an element of doubt, which he felt should be resolved.

Meanwhile, Griffiths was in Strangeways Prison, Manchester, and there during a visit by his parents, and in the presence of the Governor, he swore again that he had not committed the murder.

"I am innocent, as innocent as can be," he told them. However, on February 15th, he wrote to his mother:

"My dear Mother, I am sorry to tell you it was me that murdered my dear Katie. I hope that you will keep that photo of Katie's for my sake, and you will go and see Mrs. Garrity and tell her from me how sorry I am for what I have done. Whatever got into me to do it, I cannot say."

Despite his confession, sympathy for Griffiths was still very great, and encouraged by this, the Reverend Pinniger, Vicar of Shaw, and Mr. Morris, the Secretary of the Shaw Temperance Society, organised a public petition to reprieve Griffiths on the grounds of his youth, and also, "our belief that owing to bad home influences and degrading surroundings he had not as good a chance as ourselves."

Ten thousand signatures were obtained.

Meanwhile, Butterworth still continued to do what he could to save Griffiths's neck, and claimed that his client had told him that he had not used string to strangle Kate. His latest argument was that during a violent quarrel Kate had turned to go, so in a moment's temper Griffiths grabbed the neckband of her dress and dragged her to where her body was eventually found. A medical expert agreed with Butterworth that this action could have caused strangulation. Under these circumstances, therefore, Butterworth argued, Griffiths would be guilty only of manslaughter.

Because Griffiths had now confessed to strangling Kate, however, the Home Secretary refused to allow the new evidence.

Butterworth doggedly refused to be beaten, and asked the Bishop of Manchester to intervene. The Bishop wrote to the Home Secretary pointing out that the murder had not been premeditated and that according to the medical evidence, it had not taken more than 32 seconds to produce death. But the Home Office stood firm, stating: "There is no change in the decision."

Jack Griffiths was hanged on Tuesday, February 27th, 1906, in the morning.

Henry Pierrepoint was the executioner. The newspapers reported that although it rained continuously, it did not deter the crowd of several hundred strong from gathering outside the prison gates.

While in prison, Griffiths wrote a last letter to his mother, gravely urging her to send his brothers and sisters to Sunday School so that they would not end up like him. He assured her that he was cheerful, even going as far as to describe his stay in prison as, "the happiest I have ever been in all my life."

He seemed almost to welcome his approaching death, writing: "I hope that we shall meet in the next world, and I hope that when I leave this world for the next I shall meet my loving Katie. I will ask her to forgive me, and I hope that she will."

Whoever wrote the letter from Kent was never identified.

20
MANCHESTER'S MARSDEN SQUARE MURDER MYSTERY

Did circumstantial evidence nearly send an innocent man to the gallows?

"FIRE! THERE'S a fire!" cried a passer-by in Manchester's Marsden Square, pointing excitedly to black smoke curling from Thomas Price's warehouse. It was 1.40 p.m. on Friday, February 3rd, 1826, and several bystanders ran to alert firemen. Others dashed up the stairs of Price's warehouse to the upper sales room where the fire seemed to have started. There was not a moment to lose, as the square's warehouses were all crammed with velvets, velveteens, corduroys and other inflammable materials, and a fire here could spread rapidly.

The men who ran up the stairs to Price's upper sale room found they couldn't open the door. "Where's the key? Where's the key?" they shouted. No doubt with Mr. Price. But where was he?

Going out onto the steps of his neighbouring warehouse, Hugh Greaves saw that a large crowd had already gathered in the square. So how was it, he wondered, that Price had not yet heard of the fire? Then Greaves saw James Evans, Price's clerk, sauntering along a passage which led from Palace Street into Marsden Square. He beckoned him and Evans hurried over.

"Young man," said Greaves angrily, "you're taking things very leisurely considering the situation your master's property is in."

Evans looked surprised. "Why shouldn't I?" he asked.

"But don't you see that your warehouse is on fire? Where is Mr. Price?"

"I left him at the warehouse when I went to dinner at one," Evans replied. "He said I might go to my dinner and he would lock up."

Just then Mary Price, another employee of Thomas Price but no relation, arrived. Greaves asked her where her master was.

"He went a-collecting," she said. The first Friday of the month was the day Thomas Price collected money owing to him.

Greaves told Evans and Mary Price to try to save what they could from the fire, but Mary was soon so overcome by the smoke that she had to go and sit down in a neighbouring warehouse. As Evans worked on alone, Thomas Hudson, Price's brother-in-law, arrived. He too was concerned on learning that Price had not yet returned to the square.

"This is Mr. Price's hat," said Evans, coming out of the counting house on the first floor and showing it to Hudson. The find was disturbing because Price always wore his hat, even indoors. He was never seen without it, except on very hot days.

Hudson thought his brother-in-law might have been in the counting house, smelt smoke coming from the top floor and rushed upstairs, losing his hat on the way. But if this were so, was he still up there, trapped in the sale room?

The firemen arrived at 2.05 p.m. Putting on their leather helmets, four of them ran up to the top floor of the warehouse and attempted to open the door of the upper sale room. They failed.

"Haven't they found the key yet?" asked Hudson anxiously. Taking from his pocket a set of keys which he said he had found earlier in a drawer in the counting house, Evans handed them to Hudson, saying, "You may try to get into the room, but you can't — for I myself have tried to get up, but could not for smoke.''

Nevertheless, Hudson, with Evans following, then managed to climb the stairs despite the fumes.

They reached the upper sale room to find that James Batty, who worked in the square, had just succeeded in forcing the door, which wasn't locked. He opened it enough to get his hand through and push whatever was behind it out of the way.

"You may depend upon it, Mr. Price is dead in that room," Evans told one of the firemen. The smoke was now so thick that they could see nothing.

James Newton, another local workman, squeezed through the half-open door and crawled across the floor to the window which he smashed open, cutting his head and hands in the process. A hose was then hauled through it from the square below and within minutes the fire had been extinguished.

As the smoke began to clear the reason why the door hadn't opened became apparent. Rolls of velveteen had been piled behind it. John Read, who also worked in the square, began moving them out of the way, revealing a man's bloodstained head.

"Here's Mr. Price!" he cried. Hudson was called into the room, and although the face was badly scorched he recognised it as that of his 55-year-old brother-in-law, whose body was then carried by four firemen to the Manchester Infirmary in nearby Piccadilly.

When the surgeons had confirmed that Price was dead, Hudson went through his pockets, taking from them the key to Price's cash-drawer, a bad shilling, a few memorandums, a knife and a comb. Then he walked back to the warehouse, accompanied by Evans who said, "I should like to have a glass of ale, as I am very wet." But Hudson was thinking of his sister Alice, Price's wife, and their five children. They did not know that Price was dead, and Hudson had to go to break the news to them.

He asked Evans to remain at the warehouse until his

return, when they would sort through Price's papers. But when Hudson came back at 9 p.m. he found the warehouse locked-up. The watchman told him that the police had come and taken Evans into custody.

Deputy Constable Stephen Lavender had arrived at the warehouse at 4 p.m. after going to the infirmary where the surgeons had described Price's injuries. They had found three distinct head-wounds, including one which seemed to have been inflicted with a hammer. This blow had caused a five-inch fracture, driving the skull into the brain.

Lavender reviewed several possible explanations for Price's death. Was the fire accidental and had he died trying to save his goods? But there was no fireplace in the upper sale room, so had Price himself set the fire to claim the insurance? This seemed unlikely. Price had been a highly regarded businessman of many years standing, noted for his generosity and kindness.

The surgeons were certain that his head injuries could not have resulted from a fall had he been overcome by the smoke. And Lavender noted that Price's wig — he was completely bald — had been found almost three yards from his body. As it had no blood on it, it must have fallen off when he sustained the first two comparatively minor head wounds, and before the third, which had resulted in a heavy loss of blood.

Could one of the firemen have dealt the fatal blow with his axe as he tried to break into the room? They had all been questioned, and each had denied using his axe that day. Besides, the amount of congealed blood found in the room indicated that Price had bled onto the floorboards while they were still dry, before the firemen arrived with their hoses.

So was it murder? William Kilbie, the first policeman on the scene, had already voiced his suspicions of James Evans, who had kept coming into the upper sale room as the officer searched it, over-anxious, or so it seemed to Kilbie, about what might be found.

Mary Price, who was employed at the warehouse as an

"ender and mender," told Lavender that Mr. Price and Evans often quarrelled and that there seemed to be a hatred between them which had recently increased. This may have been due to Price's growing concern over Evans's accounting, as she had often heard her employer complain that "the figures are out."

Edward Coward, a friend of Price, had called at the warehouse on the evening prior to the fire and had found him poring over the accounts. "Never a man's stock was like mine," he had told Coward wearily. "I can't make the numbers right."

According to Mary Price, her employer had arrived at the warehouse on the day of the fire at 9.30 a.m. looking, as usual, very cheerful. He and Evans had then gone to the upper sale room, taking the stock books with them. She did not see Price again. However, she had seen a lot of Evans. He came down at 10.45 a.m. and sent her to Samuel Johnson's in Miller's Lane for a piece of corduroy. She returned 15 minutes later and was told by Evans that Price had gone out collecting.

During her absence from the warehouse, she later learned, James Brundrett, a local dyer, had called. Questioning him, Lavender discovered he had spoken to Price about the settlement of an account of £50. Price, who was alone in the upper sale room checking stock, had said, "Perhaps I can, we are going a-collecting. Call again in the afternoon, about three o'clock."

Brundrett remembered that Price was in very good spirits and, as almost always, was wearing his hat.

At 10.55 a.m. John Jackson, collecting agent for Widow Clegg and Sons, had called at the warehouse about the settlement of an account of £6. He told Lavender that he had been met on the stairs by Price, who told him to come back the next day when he would be paid.

All that morning "cutters" — much of the work in the warehouse was done by local home-workers — came to the warehouse to deliver their work or ask if any was available. Though they asked to see Price, it was always Evans who came down.

At 12 noon Evans had sent Mary to fetch a piece of fabric from the warehouse of Messrs. Heywood and Batman in nearby Milk Street. She was away 15 minutes, and on her return she found Henry Davies delivering a large supply of velveteens. He was going to leave them in the lower sale room where she was working, but she protested, "Nay, take them upstairs, there's no room here."

Davies told Lavender that, most unusually, Evans had helped him carry the material upstairs where it was placed in the upper back room. This too was unusual as it was normally put in the upper sale room, and Davies had noticed that the door to this room was shut. He did not see Price.

At 12.40 p.m. Robert Barnes, a cutter, had called at the warehouse. He told Lavender that he had gone to see Price in order to borrow 20 shillings, Price having been kind to him in the past. In the lower sale room he found Mary Price busy sewing, while Evans stood with his back to the fire picking his teeth.

"Well, Bob, what news?" Evans asked breezily. "Indifferent amongst the lower classes of people," Barnes had replied. Evans then went out and Barnes moved closer to the fire to warm himself, telling Mary that he wanted to see Mr. Price.

"You'll see him directly," she told him. But Price did not come down. As the premises were about to close for dinner, Barnes had to leave. "Shall I be able to see Mr. Price after dinner?" he asked anxiously.

"Yes, you will," promised Mary.

It was usually Mary Price's responsibility to lock up the warehouse at lunch-time, leaving the keys at the Manchester and Salford Savings Bank on the ground floor. But that day, for the first time, Evans insisted that he would lock up. Mary heard him lock the door of the upper back room — but not the upper sale room — and then come down again, the keys jangling in his hand. He then sent her out to dinner.

On her return, during the fire, she had noticed Price's hat on the desk in the counting house. It had not been there when she left for her lunch.

Lavender asked if a hammer was kept in the warehouse. Mary said there was a coal-hammer, but when she went to the drawer in the counting house where it was usually kept she found it had vanished. She was certain it had been there the previous day.

Lavender now questioned James Evans. As he did so he noticed a sprinkling of blood on the suspect's shirt-front. He wondered if Evans had cut himself shaving, but there were no marks on his face.

Asked how his shirt came to be bloodstained, Evans at first said he didn't know. Then he suggested his shirt might have got blood on it when he helped to carry Price's body to the infirmary. But the firemen told Lavender that they, and they alone, had done this and that no one had helped them.

Lavender then informed Evans that Price had apparently been murdered. And as Evans was the last person known to have been with the victim, he was taken to the police station at the New Bailey Prison where he was left in the charge of Thomas Worthington, a beadle, while Lavender continued his investigation.

As he sat by the fire Evans gloomily remarked, "If I had thought of this yesterday, I would have been in some other part of the world by this time."

Worthington asked why he wanted to run away if he were innocent.

"Oh, it's nothing but suspicion," Evans replied. "They can prove nothing against me."

Lavender had meanwhile gone to 17 Lower Byron Street, where Evans lived with his parents. Searching the suspect's bedroom, he found a small green bag containing dirty linen which included a shirt-collar and a neckcloth both apparently stained with blood.

The Evanses 15-year-old servant girl, Ann Pattison, said

that James had come in at 1.15 on the afternoon of the fire, just as she was serving dinner — she knew the time by the chiming of St. John's Church clock nearby. Pulling off his coat, James sat down immediately.

During the meal his mother and brother Tom discussed a murder which Tom had read about in that morning's paper. Mrs. Evans was eager to know more, but Tom had left the paper in his bedroom. Ann was summoned to go upstairs and get it, but James said, "Never mind, I can go for it." He was back down again in a minute, and after reading the report he returned to work.

Ann's brother James, who lived next door to the Evanses, told Lavender that after dinner that afternoon he had walked back towards his own office with Evans. They both worked in the same area, but to Pattison's surprise, Evans had suddenly veered off towards Bridge Street, which was not his usual route.

As Price was said to have gone out "collecting" before the fire, Lavender went to the firms he usually visited. None had seen Price that morning. But at John Jackson's in Cannon Street the staff recalled that Evans had called for money at 11.30 a.m.

Lavender then went to a house in Sedgwick's Court, Deansgate, where Price usually had his dinner. It was run by Jane Melbourne, a widow who eked out a living serving lunches to local businessmen. She said that Price, who had dined at her house for the last 18 months, had not been there on the day of the fire, nor had he sent word that he wouldn't be coming — as he usually did in such an event.

Lavender also spoke to Evans's father, Thomas Evans, a smallware merchant, who said that his son had worked for Price for three years and had been very happy with him. But he admitted that there had been some "bother" a short time before, when James forged a bill in Price's name. Thomas Evans himself had paid this in order to avoid his son being prosecuted.

Meanwhile, back at the warehouse, Evans's olive-green work coat had been discovered. This too had red marks on it. Hurrying back to the New Bailey, Lavender charged James Evans with Price's murder, which Evans vigorously denied.

On Saturday, February 18th, the inquest into Price's death was opened at the George and Dragon public house on Manchester's Fountain Street. It lasted three days, and the most harrowing testimony came from Kilbie, the first policeman to examine the room where Price had died.

Describing how he had found the room six inches deep in water, Kilbie said: "Taking off my gloves, I searched the water with both hands, and close to the place where Mr. Price's head had been I found a quantity of congealed blood. It was sticking to the floor and I put my fingers under it and got up as much as I could, about two pounds. The blood was stuck quite fast to the boards. In bringing up the blood I found a particle of brains."

After deliberating for 15 minutes, the jury returned a verdict of wilful murder against Evans, who was then brought into the room, looking haggard.

The coroner, Mr. John Milne, told him the jury's verdict and informed him that he was being committed to stand trial at Lancaster Assizes.

Asked if he had anything to say, Evans replied: "I am confident that no evidence has been brought before this jury that can in the least implicate me."

"That is as you think," said the coroner, "but you had better prepare yourself for the worst, for you stand in an awful position. I hope you will prove your innocence, for the sake of your own credit and for the honour of this town."

Early the next morning Evans was led out of the New Bailey Prison in leg-irons and handcuffs to a coach waiting to take him to Lancaster Castle. He was accompanied by William Kilbie and other officers, and although it was 5 a.m. a crowd had gathered to jeer him on his way.

In the coach he complained about the weight of the irons and accused Kilbie of spite in making him wear them. He seemed to know that it was Kilbie's suspicions about him which had brought him to Lavender's attention, and he abused the officer throughout the journey.

When the coach stopped at the Eagle and Child Inn at Preston, Evans was given a meal of cold roast beef which he ate heartily. But when he demanded a glass of brandy Kilbie refused. Swearing at him, Evans said that had he had a knife he would gladly have plunged it into him.

When the coach reached Lancaster the prisoner refused to get out, so he was dragged from it and then pulled through the castle gates. Once inside the prison, however, he began to tremble.

"Kilbie," he said, "I am as innocent as a babe of the murder, or of having had any hand in it. I shall call upon you at my trial to say all the stock [belonging to Price] is correct. Will you speak for me?"

"I will tell all I know about the business," Kilbie assured him.

The *Manchester Courier* suggested that Evans's bizarre behaviour on the journey to Lancaster was probably "the first stage of the drama of insanity he has been instructed to perform."

No money had been spared by the prisoner's family in obtaining lawyers to defend him, and the newspaper hinted that a plea of insanity could be expected.

But there were genuine grounds for concern about Evans's mental health.

Eighteen months earlier he had married Polly Roberts, a widow who proved to be flighty, and the marriage had been unhappy. One day he had come home early, had found her in bed with another man and had stormed out and returned to his parents' home.

During the journey to Lancaster he had told Kilbie that he wouldn't have minded being sent to the assizes if he had shot his wife and her lover. "I would gladly have hung the next day for that," he confided.

When his trial before Mr. Justice Bayley began at Lancaster Assizes on Friday, March 17th, 1826, he pleaded "Not guilty" in a firm voice, doubtless encouraged by the knowledge that the jury — unlike the one at the inquest — was made up of men who had no connection with Manchester and had read little of the newspapers there, which the defence claimed had already found him guilty.

Mary Price told the court that she left the warehouse at 1.04 on the afternoon of the fire. She knew the exact time by the clock in the square. As she left she heard someone ask if it was 1 o'clock yet, and Evans reply, "Yes." She knew Evans's voice, but she said the other was unfamiliar to her.

Evans in his statement, which was now read out in court, said it was Mr. Price who had asked him the time, and it was Price who had then taken the warehouse keys from him: otherwise, he would have left them as usual at the savings bank on the ground floor.

Evans's statement went on to say that on leaving the warehouse he had met his friend James Holman in nearby York Street. It was then 1.06 p.m. After chatting with him for a moment, Evans had hurried to his home, at least a mile away, arriving at 1.15 p.m.

This meant he could not have been in the warehouse longer than 30 seconds after Mary Price had left it. So how could he in that short time — as the prosecution claimed — have murdered Price, put his body by the door, piled rolls of velveteen on top of him — balancing two in such a way that when he closed the door they would fall, wedging it shut — and then set the fire? Besides, the bank on the ground floor was full of people at that time of day, who would surely have heard a blow or a fall.

Evans claimed that at 1.45 p.m. he had made his way back to the warehouse. As he did so he met his nephew John Lee, who told him that there was a fire at Price's warehouse and that a key was needed to open the door to the upper sale room.

Evans said he was so shocked by this news that he raced across Market Street, then down Palace Street and finally through an entry which led into Marsden Square. It was then that he met Greaves, who had testified he had seen him walking slowly.

The truth, Evans protested, was that the square was packed with people staring at the fire and he could move only at a snail's pace as he weaved his way through them, getting to the warehouse as quickly as he was able. Going into the counting house on the lower floor to save what he could from the fire, he had found the keys to the warehouse in a drawer. Remembering a key was wanted, he had then attempted to go upstairs, but was unable to do so because of the dense smoke.

He said that had he been the murderer he would have known the door wasn't locked; and the "blood" found on his clothing was red ink used at the warehouse. [At that time there was no reliable test to identify bloodstains.]

Evans also said he had no reason to kill Price, who had been more like a friend to him than an employer. There had been no money in the warehouse because Price had been sending people away all that morning who had called for payment. "Men," Evans declared, "don't commit murder at the hazard of their lives, without some mercenary views."

Denying that he was behind in his accounts, he claimed that his employer owed him £30 in back pay. It had been suggested that he had started the fire in order to destroy the cash books so that nobody would know of his shortcomings, but he pointed out that it was he himself who had saved them from the flames.

The prosecution argued that the amount of congealed blood found under Price's head indicated that he was probably murdered at 10.45 a.m. or 12 noon, when Mary Price was out of the warehouse. But Evans reminded the court that both Brundrett and Jackson had seen and spoken to Price during Mary's first absence from the warehouse at 10.45 a.m.

He himself had gone "collecting" at 11.30 a.m. If he were the killer, would he have left the victim's dead body in the upper sale room, to be discovered by Mary while he was away?

Mary Price, however, had earlier testified that she never went into that room.

Several people claimed they had seen Price alive after 11 a.m. Evans's father told the court he had passed through Marsden Square at 11.40 a.m. and had seen Price standing at the door of his warehouse. David Henry, a surgeon's servant who knew Price by sight, stated that he had seen him striding down Oxford Road at 12 noon; but under cross-examination he was unable to describe what the victim had been wearing.

James Hardman, a local businessman, said he had seen Price at 12.40 p.m. in Cannon Street, going in the direction of his warehouse. But the witness admitted that he didn't know Price to speak to, and prior to this he hadn't seen him for more than a year.

The court then heard the evidence of Mary Nelson, a hawker of ducks and pigeons, who had known Price for four years. She said she had called at his warehouse at 12.45 p.m. and had seen both Price and Gibson, who ran the savings bank on the ground floor. The two were standing together in the lobby of the warehouse. When she asked Price if he wished to buy something from her he had joked, "We shall hardly get water porridge if the times don't mend."

If her testimony were true, Price was alive right up to the time the warehouse closed for lunch at 1 p.m., and this again raised the question of how Evans could have had time to commit the murder and set the fire.

"I did not stop above five minutes with them," Mrs. Nelson added, "but I have no doubt that it was Mr. Price." She said she heard of the fire 90 minutes later and saw Price being carried to the infirmary. She did not tell the police about seeing him that day because someone to whom she mentioned it said she must be mistaken as Gibson had been at his home in the country that day, and had not come into Manchester until after the fire.

The witness said that when she learned that this was

untrue it was too late for her to attend the inquest. But on hearing about her evidence Evans's defence team had asked her to attend the Assizes on his behalf, and this she had agreed to do.

Gibson was not in court, but he had stated earlier that he had not seen Price at all on the day of the fire.

Mr. Charles Greswell, the house surgeon at Manchester Infirmary, testified that Price's skull fracture corresponded with the blade of the type of axe used by firemen. The witness added that it was "a matter of doubt whether the blow was given before, or recently after death." But if the amount of blood found at the scene weighed two pounds, as testified, then the victim was probably still alive when the fatal blow was delivered.

Mr. Robert Thorpe, another surgeon at the Manchester Infirmary, said that the murder weapon was least an inch broad, and could not have been an axe which would be too sharp. A third surgeon from the infirmary, Mr. Joseph Jordan, said a hammer or some instrument with a blunt edge was the most likely murder weapon.

Several witnesses of the fire, including Henry Dunbobbin and Dennis Gordon, testified that the firemen had taken their axes with them when they went into the warehouse. The court heard, however, that nobody who had been present at the door of the upper sale room had seen the axes used.

Dunbobbin and Gordon recalled that James Newton, the first man to enter the room, had bled copiously when he was led out of the warehouse, and the defence suggested that some of the blood found at the scene was his. But Newton testified that most of the blood had been shed in the window area and only a few drops had fallen into the room itself.

Dunbobbin and Gordon also said how difficult it had been to move in the square because of the onlookers attracted by the fire, and they told how Evans, despite the thick smoke, had dashed in and out of the warehouse carrying papers, books and other items to safety.

James Holman had initially been a witness for the prosecution, having noticed blood on Evans's collar when he met him in York Street. But he was now called as a defence witness, recalling that Evans had looked relaxed and unhurried when they met that afternoon. They had shaken hands and Evans had suggested they should have a glass of ale together one evening, saying sadly, "I have married a whore, which is damned unfortunate."

Holman said that on seeing the blood on Evans's collar, which was little more than a splash, he had assumed he had cut himself shaving. He now claimed that the collar Lavender had later shown him had had much more blood on it and couldn't have been the one he had seen Evans wearing.

Recalled to the witness box, Lavender said he had thoroughly examined Evans's face and neck that day and had found no cuts. The collar Evans wore when he was questioned had no blood on it at all, so he must have changed it.

The Evanses' servant, Ann Pattison, testified that she had eaten her dinner that afternoon in the kitchen, which was directly below James Evans's bedroom. Had he gone into his own room when he went up to get his brother's newspaper she would have heard him as he had boots with iron on the soles.

Recalled again to the witness box, Lavender said that Evans could have removed his boots.

John Lee told the court how he had met his great-uncle, Thomas Evans, near Marsden Square, who told him about the fire, that a key was needed, and asked him to intercept James on his way back to the warehouse from dinner.

Lee said that when he told his uncle what had happened James looked deeply shocked and both hurried down Market Street and through a passage into Marsden Square. However, they had found it very difficult to get to the warehouse because of the crowd. On finally reaching it they both tried to get up the stairs to the upper sale room, but couldn't because of the smoke.

At this point the judge interposed that Lee's testimony indicated that the front door of the warehouse was unlocked and open when Evans arrived, in which case he could not have taken the keys home with him, as the prosecution suggested.

Lee added that he did not see Evans produce any keys from his pockets.

Serjeant Cross, defending, claimed that Price, short of money, had set the fire himself in order to claim £1,000 insurance. But on being overcome by the fumes he had fallen backwards, striking his head on the door and knocking himself out. Rolls of cloth had then cascaded down on him, and in the confusion which followed the fire he was accidentally hit on the head by an axe as the firemen strove to enter the room.

The judge's summing-up was favourable to the defendant, and the jury reached their verdict without retiring. They acquitted James Evans and he was freed.

"Gentlemen," said Mr. Justice Bayley, "it is a case in which I should have felt very great hesitation in saying that the prisoner was guilty. It is now my duty to say that he is innocent."

The next day Evans and his family and friends returned to Manchester in triumph. "They were arrayed in ribbons as though they had arrived back from an election canvas," one newspaper noted disapprovingly.

The *Manchester Courier* commented: "The fact that Evans was found guilty in the Coroner's Court but innocent at the Assizes is baffling. That evidence of a circumstantial nature must often be found insufficient for the purpose of public justice is obvious enough, yet it cannot but be equally obvious that if this kind of evidence were rejected, ninety-nine murderers out of one hundred would escape with perfect impunity."

The newspaper added that it preferred the Scottish option of "Not Proven" in such cases as Evans's, rather than acquittal.

A few days later a letter from Gibson, manager of the

savings bank on the ground floor of Price's warehouse, appeared in all the Manchester newspapers. "Sir: Mary Nelson stated that she addressed herself to me at the door leading to my office, on the day the murder was committed, at 12.45 p.m., and that Mr. Price was in the lobby at the time. I most unequivocally declare, and am ready to make an oath, that I did not see Mary Nelson at any time during that day and at the time she says she addressed me I was engaged with the Committee of the Savings Bank.

"I was in the office with them from 12.30 to 1.15 p.m., and was never out of it and I did not see Mr. Price at all that day until his dead body was brought into the Savings Bank after it had been found in the top room of the warehouse. I was on very friendly terms with Mr. Price and we never saw each other without speaking."

A day or two later Mary Nelson's reply was published: "Sir: I am still (as I was at the trial of James Evans) perfectly satisfied that I saw the late Mr. Price at the time and place I stated in my evidence."

She then went on to question how Gibson, busy as he was with his committee, could say with such certainty how long he was with them, or that he didn't see Price that day.

Perhaps fearful of being charged with perjury, she added that she had several witnesses who had heard her speak of seeing Price on the day of the fire.

Her letter concluded: "I am no relation, or in any way connected or even acquainted with James Evans and I have no interest to serve by the statement I made, on the contrary, my going to Lancaster was a matter of inconvenience to me and my family."

To this day the case remains a mystery. Did Price start the fire to cash in on the insurance? Did circumstantial evidence nearly send an innocent man to the gallows? Or did James Evans get away with murder?

21
MURDER FOR OLD CLOTHES

"My life has been falsely signed away"

EVERY SUNDAY morning Joseph Cass walked down a cinder track at the Lancashire village of Birtle, near Bury, to call on his brother Benjamin, an elderly farmer who lived at the Pit House with his wife Alice. The morning of Sunday, October 2nd, 1825, was no exception, but on arriving Joseph was surprised to see that his brother's front door was ajar.

Pushing it open, he stepped inside and saw Benjamin sitting on a couch in front of the fireplace with Alice sitting next to him leaning on his shoulder. As they did not look up or appear to notice him, he said, "What, are you asleep?"

It was not until he laid his hand on his brother's head that he realised that it was covered with blood, and that Benjamin and Alice were dead.

He immediately ran to the home of John Chadwick, a neighbouring farmer, who hurried back with him to the Pit House.

Examining the dead couple, Chadwick saw that Benjamin Cass's head was leaning against the back of the sofa and his feet were stretched out in front of him against the fender. Alice's head was resting on her husband's right shoulder, her arms dangling limply. On the floor near the couch lay a large stick, a small poker, and part of an old spade which appeared to have been used in the house as a coal-shovel. The head of the spade had been worn away, but the edges were sharp and it looked a formidable weapon. The stick did not appear to have been used, but the spade and the poker were covered with blood and the grey hairs of the two victims.

The room had been ransacked, but at first nothing seemed to have been taken, and 13 shillings in silver lay in full view in a bedroom upstairs.

Some of the couple's clothes were missing, however, and three days later 26-year-old John Diggles, an unemployed cotton weaver, was arrested at the Blue Bell Inn, Royton. He had been accosted by a man who, recognising Benjamin Cass's coat, said, "Isn't that the old man's coat you've got on?"

Diggles had no answer, and after being questioned by Constable Jonathan Chadwick he was placed in the Lock-Up House at Royton.

Sandy-haired and blue-eyed, Diggles stepped into the dock at Lancaster Assizes on March 17th, 1826, charged with the couple's murder and with robbing them.

Pleading not guilty, he said he would be tried by God and his country.

"God send you a safe deliverance," said the court's clerk.

A surgeon from Bury, Joseph Goodlad, told the court he had been called to examine the victims shortly after their bodies were found. Mr. Cass had suffered several vicious cuts with the spade, one of which had split his nose. None of these had been fatal, but both victims had fractured skulls, which had caused their deaths. These injuries had been inflicted, the doctor thought, with a blunt poker. As there was no evidence of a struggle, the couple had probably died instantaneously.

The surgeon added that he believed that two killers were involved because the spade had been wielded by a hand weaker or less determined than the hand that had used the poker.

The next witness was Richard Brierly, who said that at

about 3.30 p.m. on October 1st he had been travelling on the road from Bury towards Haslingden, when he saw Diggles with another man, Ralph Weston, whom he knew by sight.

Another witness, John Quick, said that on the same day he saw Diggles at about 5 p.m. walking towards Bury. He was on his own, and didn't appear to be carrying anything.

Samuel Sladden testified that he was on the road from Rochdale to Halifax on the night of October 1st when he overtook a man walking alone. The man, whom he now identified in court as Diggles, had two bundles over his shoulder and an umbrella. In passing, Diggles had remarked, "Well, old man, it is a fine night," and then asked if Sladden would like to buy a pair of stockings.

Diggles had then placed one of his bundles on a wall, opened it and displayed several pairs, Sladden buying them all for 2s 8d. The two had then gone to a cinder oven where Diggles showed Sladden another pair of stockings.

Sladden told the court that when he arrived home he gave the stockings to his sister. A fortnight later, on hearing of the Birtle murders, he handed them to Constable Taylor. He added that he had stayed with Diggles until 6 a.m. They had parted after drinking two pints of ale at the "Sign of the Gate" on the Halifax road.

Diggles jumped to his feet on hearing this evidence, protesting: "Sladden was a prisoner himself in Manchester Prison for six weeks and he is swearing my life away!"

Questioned by the judge, Sladden admitted being a thief, and having stolen four bricks.

John Ashworth, a cotton spinner at Royton, said he had seen Diggles in the Unicorn public house on the morning of October 3rd, offering his shoes for sale.

Diggles had said his shoes were too small and he wanted to exchange them with somebody. He wanted four shillings, but Ashworth offered him two. They bartered, and finally Diggles agreed to accept two shillings, a quart of beer and Ashworth's own shoes. While still at the pub, Diggles sold an umbrella to a man named Cordingly for 1s. 6d.

John Wilde, the next witness, said he too was at the pub, and he bought a suit from Diggles for 12 shillings, later discovering a pair of spectacles in the waistcoat pocket.

Constable Chadwick told the court he had arrested Diggles after being dissatisfied with his account of how he obtained Benjaming Cass's coat. Diggles had said he'd bought it between Prescot and St. Helens.

William Cass, Benjamin's nephew, testified that he had made shoes for his uncle but had never made any for Diggles, whom he had known since he was a boy. The shoes Diggles had sold in the Unicorn, said the witness, were a pair he himself had made for his uncle.

Thomas Cramplin, a tailor, said he had examined the suit sold by Diggles to John Wilde and he recognised it as one he had made for Benjamin Cass. He had made the breeches two or three years ago from material Cass himself had supplied. He had not made the coat, but had lengthened the sleeves and made other alterations.

The spectacles found in the waistcoat of the suit sold by Diggles were identified as Benjamin's by his neighbour, West Howard. And James Ashworth said that he recognised the umbrella sold by Diggles. It was his own — he had left it at Cass's house some weeks earlier.

The next witness was Joseph Coats, who had been in custody with Diggles at Royton. He said that Diggles had told him he had become friendly with Ralph Weston, and on the day of the murder they had gone to Birtle. When they got there Weston had said he was going to see if he could get some money, and when Diggles asked him how, Weston had just smiled and tapped the end of his nose.

"You mean steal it?" Diggles said he had asked. Telling Diggles to wait for him in a nearby meadow, he disappeared down the road. When he returned he was carrying a bundle of clothes and other items which he split between himself and his friend.

Diggles had noticed there was blood on Weston's hands. "Thou hasn't killed anyone, hast thou?" Diggles had asked. But Weston had replied that he had merely hurt his victims a little when they had tried to hinder his escape.

According to Diggles, the two had then parted company and he had gone on his way to Halifax.

Coats testified that he had reported this conversation to the police and Weston had been arrested and brought to the jail to see Diggles. Coats said he was present and claimed he had overheard their conversation.

"Did thou tell them it was I who murdered Benjamin Cass?" Weston had demanded.

"No," Diggles told him. "But I will and I'll swear to it an' all."

"But thou knows thou'd be telling lies," shouted Weston. "I was at Barton that night and I've witnesses to prove it."

"Then all you have to do, my friend, is find them," Diggles had replied. "But come, don't make thisel uneasy. Nobody yet knows of it but we two."

As Coats concluded his evidence, Diggles, again sprang to his feet. "But his words are false," he protested. "I said nowt of the kind."

Ralph Weston had apparently found his witnesses and the police had been satisfied with his alibi, for he had been released and he was not called to testify.

The court heard that Diggles had also been found in possession of Alice Cass's shawl, and it took the jury only 30 minutes to decide that he was guilty.

Sentenced to death, he mounted the scaffold at Lancaster Castle a few days later, still protesting, "My life has been falsely sworn away."

22
WARRINGTON'S FIRST EVER MURDER INVESTIGATION

Pub landlady raped and slain in the privy

WHEN A policeman cracks a murder mystery and brings the killer to justice he can expect congratulations from the judge and a commendation from his superiors. But it wasn't always like that. Not when James Jones, Deputy Constable of Warrington, Lancashire, brought the town's first police investigation of a murder to a successful conclusion. Instead of congratulating him the trial judge reprimanded him for being too inquisitive!

The crime scene was a Warrington pub, the Legh Arms, where buxom, middle-aged Betty Minshull presided over the bar and stood no nonsense. She was the landlord's 52-year-old married daughter, and she had come from Manchester to help her father run the inn following the death of her mother.

Eighteen months later, at closing-time in the early hours of Friday, December 8th, 1837, she was seeing the last remaining customer off the premises when he suddenly threw his arms around her. But Betty wasn't alarmed. She was used to customers becoming over-affectionate when they'd had a drink too many. She'd handled such situations before.

"Now, lad, it's time thee went home," she said as she gently tried to free herself from the young man's embrace. But his grip round her shoulders only tightened, and the look in his drink-sodden eyes became menacing.

A moment later he was forcing her across the back yard to the small lean-to privy. And there, with his lips pressed roughly against hers, he began pulling up her skirts.

Betty screamed, but who would hear her at 1 o'clock on that cold December morning? Most of the other pubs in the town-centre had closed, and their staff had gone to bed. Freeing her arms, Betty lashed out at the man, tearing his face with her fingernails. But big though she was, she was no match for him, and he soon overpowered her and raped her. She screamed again — the worst thing she could have done, for he responded by putting both his hands round her throat and squeezing long and hard until she lay dead.

Then he raped her again and turned out her pockets, removing her silver-coloured snuff-box, her small, bone-handled knife and the pub's takings for that night. Having pocketed the cash, the snuff-box and the knife, he rose to his feet and left through the back yard's door and the passage beyond it.

But somebody else was still up and about. Standing at the bottom of the entry was Isaac Bellass, just back from a spree and hammering on the door of his lodgings. He looked round at the man hurrying towards him down the passage.

"Bill," he said, "is that thee?" But to Isaac's surprise the man brushed past him without a word and made off towards Horsemarket Street.

Fast asleep in the bedroom she shared with Betty, Mary Pritchard was woken by the watchman calling the hour at 5 a.m. She was the pub's housemaid, and of necessity an early-riser. Sitting up, she lit a candle, glanced at Betty's bed and was startled to see that it hadn't been slept in.

Where could Betty be? The previous evening had been a busy one. It was the last night of Warrington's eight-day Winter Fair, which attracted thousands who came to buy or sell horses, to hire labour or just to have a good time. The pubs had been packed, their staff run off their feet, and Betty had told Mary she was glad the fair was at last over.

There had still been customers in the pub when Mary retired at midnight, and Betty, looking tired, had said she would soon be closing. But where was she now? Suddenly Mary remembered that Mrs. Minshull was subject to occasional fits. So was she lying downstairs unconscious?

Taking her candle, Mary went down to see. There was no sign of Betty, but the back door, which opened onto the yard, was wide open. Mary hurried out and crossed the yard to the privy.

Suppressing a scream as she saw Betty lying on the floor, her skirts rucked up above her knees, Mary knelt and touched her. The marble coldness of Betty's skin left no doubt that she was dead. Mary pulled her friend's skirts back into position and ran to wake Tom Higginson, Betty's father.

Weeping uncontrollably as he watched two of his lodgers carry his daughter into the pub, he said she must have died during one of her fits, and he began to make preparations for the funeral. Betty's inside-out pockets and the absence of the previous night's takings seemed to go unnoticed. Perhaps everyone was too distressed.

Others who knew Betty said she must have eaten one pie too many — she had a reputation for gluttony. But Alice Thomas had other ideas. She was the landlady of the Barley Mow next door to the Legh Arms, and she recalled that on retiring for the night at 1 o'clock that morning she had been startled by screams which came from behind the Legh Arms. She had looked out of her bedroom window, which overlooked the back yards of both pubs, but could see nothing.

"From the screams," she told her customers, "it seemed as if someone was abusing a female." Although her daughter and servant were with her, she said, she was afraid to go out, so she had closed her window and gone to bed. But now, on hearing that Betty Minshull had been found dead in the privy next door, she was putting "two and two together."

When this reached the ears of James Jones, the town's recently appointed Deputy Constable, he went to investigate. Mr. Higginson, convinced that his daughter had been carried off by one of her fits or by "wind striking down to her heart," reluctantly allowed the policeman to view the body.

Seeing bruises on Betty's throat and two scratches which could have been made by fingernails under her chin, Jones said he would inform the coroner and there would be a post-mortem examination.

Mr. Higginson was upset. He didn't mind an inquest, he said, but he didn't like the thought of Betty being cut up. Jones warned him that if he went ahead and buried her a coroner's order would be obtained to have her exhumed.

When the autopsy was carried out by Dr. John Davies on the morning of December 11th both sides of Betty's neck were found to be swollen and the muscles badly bruised. There was also severe bruising on her forearms, particularly above the elbows and wrists, and when her chest was opened the blood in her lungs indicated that she had died from strangulation.

That afternoon, after hearing this medical evidence, the inquest jury returned the verdict that Betty Minshull had "come to her death by violent means, under circumstances unknown." And James Jones found himself leading the first murder inquiry to be conducted by Warrington's recently formed constabulary. London's metropolitan police force was less than 10 years old, and county constabularies and the first provincial city police force in Birmingham had yet to be established.

Once Mr. Higginson and Mary Pritchard had accepted that Betty had been murdered they began to realise the significance of several things they had forgotten in the confusion which followed the discovery of her body. Mr. Higginson now remembered that the evening's takings were missing. Betty had always put copper coins in the drawer in the bar, keeping silver in her apron pocket for safety, and subsequently transferring the takings to a drawer in her father's bedroom. The pub had been busy that Thursday evening, the last of the fair, but no silver had been found in Betty's pockets or in Mr. Higginson's bedroom.

After Betty's body was discovered the back yard door, which Mr. Higginson always locked before going to bed, had been found open, its padlock and key flung to one side. And Mary Pritchard told Jones that when she found Betty her skirts had been pulled up above her knees, and her corset stays had been twisted and bent back. The girl also recalled that Betty's pockets had been turned inside-out and her snuff-box and small knife — used for cutting lemons in the bar — were both missing and nowhere to be found.

Asked who had been in the pub on the night in question, Mary said about eight regular customers were in the tap-room. She remembered that they included James Kerfoot, Peter Gleave, John Boardman, Joseph Yates, William Hill, Edward Cox and James Holbrook. Joking, laughing and singing, they had also done a lot of drinking. In addition to a free half-gallon of ale, Mrs. Minshull had given them a quart Mr. Higginson had sent over for them, and they themselves had bought at least another half-gallon.

Later in the evening William Hill had stood up and had sung several songs. He had a fine voice, and Betty had appeared to be very taken with it. She had subsequently sat chatting with him for at least an hour. Asked if Mrs. Minshull had been drinking, Mary said, "No."

Jones next questioned James Holbrook, a cotton weaver who had been one of the company. He said that at 12.30 a.m Edward Cox and Joseph Yates had suddenly begun quarrelling. Mrs. Minshull never tolerated fighting on the premises, and she told them to leave. They had stumbled out into the Market Place where, egged on by the others who had followed them, they had fought briefly and then gone home.

At the same time Mrs. Minshull had taken the opportunity to close the pub for the night. Holbrook recalled that only one of her customers had remained — William Hill. A 27-year-old weaver, Hill worked with Holbrook at Cockhedge Mill in Cockhedge Lane, and earlier in the evening he and Mrs. Minshull had taken it in turns to sing.

Holbrook said that at about 11.50 he had been sitting between Hill and Mrs. Minshull when she went to fetch a fresh supply of ale. During her absence Hill, by now drunk, had nudged him, saying, "I will — that old woman before I go home."

Holbrook also recalled glancing back at the pub as he left, and seeing Hill and Mrs. Minshull standing together near the door as she closed it. When Hill arrived at work at 6 a.m. Holbrook had asked him how much longer he had stayed at the pub, and Hill had replied, "I stayed about twenty minutes and then left."

Holbrook also told Jones he had noticed that Hill had four deep scratches on his left cheek, which had not been there the previous evening.

Holbrook's sister Eliza had been in the Legh Arms briefly that Thursday evening, and she told Jones that it was she who the following afternoon had broken the news to Hill that Betty Minshull was dead. She said he had looked shocked, exclaiming, "Aye, by God, is hoo [she]?"

"What time did you get home last night?" Eliza had asked him.

"I don't know," he had replied, "but there was a row between them [Cox and Yates] and I helped Mrs. Minshull to get them away. I then went in with her, we drank the drink which was left and I stopped in with her for a quarter of an hour."

"Who has scratched your face?" Eliza had asked.

Hill told her he got the scratches when he intervened in the fight, but James Holbrook later told Jones that Hill had not involved himself in the brawl.

By this time Isaac Bellass had come forward. He told

Jones that at about 1.30 a.m. on the Friday he had seen William Hill hurry down the passage from the back yard of the Legh Arms. He knew Hill well, he added; on the Wednesday night they had gone to a circus together.

On December 12th, five days after the murder, Jones arrested William Hill and took him to the police station in Dial Street. In a statement Hill said that after he had helped Mrs. Minshull to eject the men in the pub who were fighting she had said to him, "There's some ale left in the jug, Bill; you may as well drink it."

"I said, 'No, I don't want any more at present,'" his statement continued. "But she said, 'You may as well drink it, it will only spoil before morning and will do us no good.' So I took hold of the glass and drank it. Then she says, 'There's another glass in.' But I said, 'Well, never mind, you drink that.'

"But she replied, 'No, drink it yourself.' Then she said she did not like fighting and I said, 'No, it's very disagreeable.' Then I took hold of the other glass and drank that. She supped a sup of it and I took the rest. Then she went with me to the front door, with a glass in one hand and a lighted candle in the other.

"She says, 'I think they're all gone.' I said, 'I think they are.' Then she said, 'Good night,' and I said 'Good night.' It was about a quarter of an hour after the men had left the pub."

With insufficient evidence to justify detaining Hill for further questioning, Jones had to let him go. If only, he thought, he could find Mrs. Minshull's snuff-box or her little knife. Hill's home in Cockhedge Lane, where he lived with his widowed mother, and his work-place had been searched without success.

Then on December 22nd the deputy constable was visited by Richard Lyon, an overlooker at the mill where Hill worked. They were great friends, Lyon told Jones, and that was why he had hesitated for some time before approaching the police. But now his conscience would let him remain silent no longer.

He said that at 3 a.m. on Friday, December 8th, he had been roused by loud and persistent knocks on his front door in Strang Lane. He opened it to find Hill standing outside. Although Hill had some nasty scratches on his face he seemed very cheerful, saying he had been to the fair the previous evening and had later had sex with a landlady — "The best lark of my life!"

Hill had then produced a small bone-handled knife from his pocket, giving it to Lyon as a keepsake and asking Lyon to wake him on his way to work a few hours later, as he thought he might oversleep. Lyon had said he would do so. Apart from the scratches on his face, the overlooker told Jones, his friend had seemed much as usual.

But the following morning, before any of the men had been paid, Hill had suddenly handed Lyon a half-sovereign and six shillings in silver, asking him to keep the money for him until Christmas. He did not say how he had come by it.

As Lyon continued his story Jones listened with increased interest. The half-sovereign and six shillings added up to the amount Mr. Higginson had calculated was missing from his pub's takings.

The overlooker said that later on that Saturday, when his friend had asked him to look after the money, Hill had needed to trim some threads. He had asked Lyon for the knife he had given him the previous morning. The overlooker had handed it to him, and Hill had never returned it.

Lyon went on to say that on the morning of Monday, December 11th — by which time all Warrington knew of Betty Minshull's murder — he noticed that Hill seemed agitated, and kept bringing up the subject of Mrs. Minshull's death. Then when he and the overlooker were alone he blurted out that she was the woman he'd had sex with on Friday morning.

Hill had said he had stayed on at the Legh Arms after everyone else had left, and he and Mrs. Minshull had drunk a couple of glasses of ale together. Then she had told him she would let him out by the back yard door, but when they got to the bottom of the yard he had grabbed her and pushed her into the privy. She had tried to fight him off, screaming and scratching his face, but he'd had sex with her twice, the second time while she was "asleep."

Going through her pockets, he had taken a snuff-box and a small knife — the one he had given Lyon later that same morning, but had since taken back. Hill said he had now thrown it into the nearby reservoir, and he was going to do the same with the snuff-box. Taking it from his pocket, he showed it to Lyon, who saw that it looked like silver, had a ribbed surface and the number 66 inside it. Later, at 9.30 a.m., Hill had told the overlooker he had now flung the snuff-box into the reservoir.

On December 22nd, as snow fell around them, Jones and Assistant Constable Tom Joynson watched workmen dam and then drain the part of the reservoir where Hill had told Lyon he had thrown the snuff-box.

The workmen searched for hours without success. Then, just as the temporary dam was about to give way, one of them saw something glinting in the mud. Grabbing it, he leapt to safety just as the water flooded back into the area. On examining the find Jones saw it was a silver-coloured snuff-box with a ribbed surface and "66" stamped inside it.

Three months later, on Thursday, March 29th, 1838, William Hill pleaded not guilty when he appeared before Mr. Justice Patteson at Liverpool Assizes, charged with Betty Minshull's murder.

Deputy Constable Jones told the court: "After I arrested Hill I asked him where he went to when he left Mr. Higginson's on the early morning of Friday, December 8th, and he said he went home. I asked him if he saw any person on his way home. He replied, 'No, not any.'

"I asked him who slept with him that night. He said his brother James. I asked him if anyone heard him come into the house. He said he could not tell. I afterwards saw several scratches on his left cheek and one under his left ear and asked him how he had got them. He replied that he thought they were done in the row at Higginson's.''

At this point Mr. Brandt, defending, raised an objection, asking the judge if this part of the policeman's evidence was admissible. Mr. Justice Patteson said it most certainly was not. Rounding on the deputy constable, he told him: "It is a very wrong thing. Leave off this practice immediately, Mr. Jones, and don't presume to ask questions of prisoners in your custody which you have no right whatsoever to put. If you persist in doing this sort of thing, I shall strongly recommend that you be turned out of the police directly."

It was one thing for a suspect to volunteer information and to be questioned about it, the judge said, but quite another for him to be interrogated. "It is not your duty," he warned Jones, "but contrary to your duty." [Police forces were at that time in their infancy, their powers yet to be clearly defined.]

Hill's companions at the Legh Arms on the night in question all swore that he had not intervened in the fight between Cox and Yates, and had not left with them when they departed.

Repeating the story he had told Jones, Richard Lyon testified that although Hill had never admitted to him that he had strangled Betty Minshull, he had confessed to raping her twice, the second time while she was "asleep." Handed the snuff-box recovered from the reservoir, he identified it as the one Hill had shown him.

Mary Pritchard identified it as Mrs. Minshull's. It was not silver but tin, the court heard, and was worth only a few pennies.

Mr. Brandt, describing Betty Minshull as "a woman of corpulent habits," suggested that her death was natural and inevitable in view of her huge appetite. Even if Hill had raped her, the defence counsel argued, he had not meant to kill her, and he should therefore be convicted only of manslaughter. Later on the morning of Mrs.

Minshull's death, Mr. Brandt added, Hill would hardly have told Richard Lyon what he had been doing if he thought she was dead.

Summing-up, the judge told the jury that if they believed that Hill had intended to rape Mrs. Minshull, and she died as a consequence, it was a case of murder. But if they thought she had agreed to have sex with him and the violence used was part of the act consented to, then it was a case of manslaughter.

After retiring for an hour and 10 minutes the jury found William Hill guilty of murder. Sentencing him to death, Mr. Justice Patteson told him that although he didn't think he had intended to kill Betty Minshull when he went out into the yard with her, he believed he had meant to rape her.

As the death sentence was pronounced Hill closed his eyes and swayed slightly. Then he recovered and walked from the dock unaided.

Many Warrington residents signed a petition seeking a reprieve on the grounds that Hill had not intended to murder Mrs. Minshull, and the rector of Warrington wrote a letter in the same vein to Mr. Justice Patteson.

The long delay which followed before the execution date was announced gave Hill and his supporters false hope, but this was completely dashed on April 19th when it was announced that the court's decision had been upheld.

Shortly before he went to the gallows Hill admitted raping Betty Minshull, emphasising that she had not encouraged his advances. He said he could not remember strangling her and he had not realised she was dead when he left her.

At 8 a.m. on Saturday, April 21st, 1838, he mounted the scaffold outside Liverpool's Kirkdale Prison, watched by 5,000 spectators. But as the noose was being placed around his neck a man rushed forward from the crowd clutching a letter which he thrust into the hands of the prison chaplain.

Seeing that it bore the words "To be delivered instantly — affecting life and death," the chaplain thought it must be a last-minute reprieve. To shouts from the crowd of "Stop! Stop the execution!" he tore the letter open. For a moment it seemed, as one newspaper put it, that "on the edge of the grave itself salvation had arrived."

But it was no reprieve, merely a note asking for the execution to be stayed on the grounds of Hill's innocence, and the chaplain had to tell Hill his hanging must proceed.

Seconds later William Hill was dead. "Nobody is to blame but myself," he had told a friend only hours earlier. "I was always ready for anything that was bad."

23

THE BROTHERS' REVENGE

"We never thought what a crime we were committing, nor the consequences of it"

T HE DAVIES family had just settled round the fire in the drawing-room of their home at Little Hough, near Crewe, on a stormy evening in January, 1890, when the door burst open and 16-year-old George came running in. "Quick! Quick!" he shouted. "You've got to come! Something dreadful's happening. Pa's being attacked in Crewe Lane by two men!"

His mother and sister Emily threw down their needlework and jumped to their feet.

"No, you stay here," said George's 18-year-old brother Richard. "I'll go with George and see what's happening."

The two lads hurried off to the home of their elder brother John, nearby. And John, lantern in hand, went with them to investigate.

Their progress down the lane was hindered not only by the dark — it was now well past eleven o'clock — but also by the gale that was sweeping across the Cheshire countryside. The wind was so strong that they had to take a step back for every two steps forward. At last, however, they battled their way to the spot where Richard's trap stood, wind-buffeted, abandoned and ponyless in the lane.

Searching around by the flickering light of the lantern, they found their 51-year-old father lying dead at the side of the road, his head bludgeoned.

As Richard went to fetch the police, John asked George to repeat his account of what had happened.

The boy said that he and his father had left their shop in Crewe, as usual, at ten o'clock that evening, setting out for their home three miles away.

Apart from the storm, the journey had been uneventful until they turned into Crewe Lane. There two men had suddenly jumped out from the hedge on each side and seized the pony's head, stopping it in its tracks.

George had tried unsuccessfully to urge the animal on with his whip, and had then leapt from the trap in fright. He saw one of the men dash at his father and strike him on the head, dragging him from the trap and onto the road.

George said that the man who had been holding the pony then left it and chased him up the lane for about 400 yards. But after failing to catch him, had turned back to his companion who was wrestling with Richard Davies Snr. on the ground. George had run home and raised the alarm.

When the police arrived George said that because it had been so dark he could only give vague descriptions of the two men. One was big and the other small, and the man who chased him wore dark clothes and a flat-topped stiff hat. One of the men had a large walking stick.

At first, robbery was thought to be the motive for the attack. Davies was a tailor who owned four shops in Crewe and was known to carry large sums of money. On that particular evening, however, he had only £10. This was taken, but his valuable watch and chain had not been touched.

With daylight the full extent of the struggle became apparent. There was blood on the grass on both sides of the lane, and Davies had evidently tried to escape by trying to crawl through gaps in the hedge.

Doctors Matthews and Travis arrived and concluded that the victim's head injuries had been inflicted with something sharp, because he had a deep gash above his eyes. There were also three cuts on the right side of his forehead, each nearly an inch wide and of equal length, as if made with a chopper.

The back of his head was smashed in, and when a cloth covering his body was lifted, part of his skull fell away.

Searching for clues, the police discovered footprints leading in the direction of Crewe Station. But Superintendent Leah had noted several inconsistencies in George Davies' story. At first the superintendent put this down to shock, but then evidence came to light which changed the entire course of the investigation.

Some of the victim's wounds appeared to have been caused by a sharp cutting instrument, others by something blunt, and Leah learned that a small hatchet with a hammer on one side and a blade on the other had disappeared from the dead man's principal shop.

It was used for chopping fire-wood, and an assistant at the shop remembered seeing it in the yard at 5 p.m. on the day of the murder. On the next day he noticed it was missing.

Leah interviewed the Davies family at their home and learned that Richard, like his younger brother, worked in the shop in Crewe. He had arrived home only minutes before George came running in with the news of the attack on their father.

A search in Richard's bedroom uncovered an overcoat and gaiters which both had blood on them. Richard had not been wearing either when he had gone with the others to look for his father, nor had he been wearing them when he went to fetch the police.

There was also a large amount of money in the pocket of the overcoat which Richard was unable to account for.

It now seemed to Leah that two of the brothers must have been involved in their father's murder. But what could have been their motive? Money?

Although their father had once been wealthy, due to his heavy gambling his four shops were heavily mortgaged. So could the motive be revenge?

At her husband's inquest Mrs. Davies said that her

family were happy. But further investigation proved this to be untrue. Davies, the police learned from neighbours, was often unduly harsh with his wife and children, and Mrs. Davies, particularly, had suffered abuse and beatings.

Leah was now confident that he knew the motive for the killing, and interrogated both brothers again.

At first they denied having anything to do with the murder, but when they were arrested and taken to the police station they broke down and made full confessions.

George, described by his family as sullen, said: "On Saturday, January 25th, 1890, my brother Richard took me to one side and said. 'I tell you what I think. I shall have a go at the old chap tonight and I think I shall use that little chopper in the yard.'

" 'No, I shouldn't.' I warned him. 'It would be missed.' But Richard went on. 'You won't see me after I've hit him, I shall go home and you must come round about ten minutes later and say that Father has been attacked.'

"We parted, and I thought no more about it. I did not think he would do it. Then at about 10.35 p.m., just as we got into Crew Lane, Dick came out from the hedge and leapt onto the trap, hitting father with something. 'Oh dear, what's that?' Pa said. Dick hit him again, and he fell out of the back of the trap. The pony had gone on a bit, so I got out and went down the lane and waited there.

"Dick then went home first and, as he'd told me to, I waited ten minutes and then went running into the house to tell them Pa had been attacked."

Richard's confession gave a significantly different account of the night's events. "I hereby confess that me and my brother George made it up to kill father on Saturday, January 25th, 1890. I left the shop at about eight o'clock to go home.

"Instead of going home, I went and hid in Crew Lane to wait for Pa to come. When he did, I leapt out from the hedge and seized the pony's head, while George, who had the axe from the shop, struck Pa hard with it. After George had hit Pa two or three times, I ran behind and caught hold of Pa and pulled him out of the trap. When I had, George got out of the trap and then I went home. He came in ten minutes later, as we arranged, saying father had been attacked by two men."

Richard added that he and George had attacked their father because "Pa was so bad, not to me so much but to George and the others."

He said that his father was also a bad husband to their mother, and when he was in a temper, which was often, he would refuse to buy the family either coal for the fire or meat to eat.

"Sometimes we very nearly starved, but we never thought what a crime we were committing, nor the consequences of it, and I hope the law will be merciful to me and to George."

George was furious when this statement was read out to him. "Tell the truth," he screamed at his brother. "You had the axe, and you know it!"

"It is all as I have written it," said Richard firmly.

"No!" shouted George, trying to get at his brother.

"Yes!" Richard shouted back. "You came to me with the axe and said if I didn't finish him with it, you would, and you struck him on the side of the head."

"I never struck him and you know it. I never handled the axe," yelled George.

They were then returned to their cells before they came to blows.

Though their confessions were later retracted, both were charged with their father's murder and brought to trial on March 17th, 1890, at Chester Assizes.

Dressed in black, Mrs. Davies described her husband's brutality towards herself and their six children. She said he had often beaten her in the presence of her children, and had once attempted to set fire to her bed by lighting papers underneath it.

She claimed he had also pointed guns at her, threatening to shoot her, and treated the children just as badly. He would often beat them for no reason, and on Sundays, instead of being allowed to attend church, the boys were forced to work on the farm at their home.

Mrs. Davies testified that the family were also kept short of money due to Davies's meanness and gambling, and — from the evidence of letters discovered shortly before his murder — his habit of keeping other women.

Richard and George were both good sons, she insisted.

"Did Richard ever come down from his bed to save you from your husband's violence?" asked his defence counsel.

"Yes, he told me to come away from him."

"I believe on other occasions also, Richard has saved you from your husband?"

"Yes."

George told the court that he had never once dined with his father, who would not tolerate his eating in the same room with him.

Asked why he had not left home, George said he was afraid his father would have brought him back and made his life even more miserable.

Although Richard still insisted that George had killed their father, the medical evidence did not support this. Dr. Mathews produced diagrams showing that the fatal blows had all been dealt on Davies's right side. As George had been seated on his father's left — witnesses had seen them leaving Crewe — George could not have been responsible for the lethal wounds.

After retiring for about an hour the jury convicted both brothers, and they were sentenced to death. A newspaper reported: "They wrung their hands and sobbed piteously, giving way to uncontrollable grief."

After much petitioning, George's sentence was eventually commuted to penal servitude for life on account of his extreme youth and the fact that Dr. Mathews's evidence indicated that he had not struck the fatal blows.

But there was no reprieve for Richard, who was executed at Knutsford on April 8th, 1890.

"I truthfully declare in my last hour that I never struck my father on the night of his death, and that I never had the axe in my hand," he said in his last statement.

George served his sentence in Strangeways Prison, Manchester and was released in March 1905, when he was 31.

24

"HE'S ONLY A BOBBY"

Did Mary jump or was she pushed?

THE PILE of clothes that nearly sent John Green sprawling lay on the ground by the Manchester, Bolton and Bury Canal at Pendleton, near Salford. It was 7 a.m. on St. Valentine's Day, 1863, when he tripped over them in the early morning gloom as he hurried along the canal's towpath. Examining them, he found they were a nightdress, skirt, crinoline, cloak and a nightcap in which five pennies were wrapped in scraps of paper. As the clothes were so near the water, Green suspected their owner had drowned herself, so he ran to the nearest house.

The door was opened by William Gardner, a carpenter, who accompanied Green to the towpath, taking along his grappling-iron to explore the murky water. Soon the grappling-iron's rope became taut, and with helpers Gardner hauled the partly clothed body of a young woman from the canal. The police were notified and the corpse was taken to the Church Inn in Albert Street. A doctor was called, and he said the woman had not been in the water for many hours. Although she had a large bruise on one of her arms, he did not suspect foul play, as there were no other marks of violence on her body.

An inquest jury returned an open verdict of "found drowned," and four days later the unknown woman was buried in a pauper's grave at Salford Borough Cemetery. Her description was circulated to local police stations in an effort to identify her, and her clothes were kept at Salford Workhouse in case anyone came forward.

Several months were to pass before the dead woman was identified. Meanwhile a curious scene took place a few miles away, at a police constable's lodgings in Bury. Hearing a knock at his door, PC Luke Charles found that the caller was his wife's sister, Miss Julia Dunn, and she was angry. "Where's my sister?" she demanded. "I hear you've just come back from Ireland. Have you brought Mary back with you?"

"Oh, she's here," the constable told her.

"Where?" asked Miss Dunn, putting her foot in the door.

"I can't tell you."

"Why not?"

"She's told me I mustn't, that's why," said PC Charles, pushing his sister-in-law back into the street and slamming his door.

Miss Dunn was irate. It was now May, and she hadn't seen her sister since January. But several more months were to pass before, becoming increasingly suspicious, she went to Bury police station, where she was shown into the office of Superintendent Andrew Milne, head of the Bury division.

"All I want to know is where my sister has gone," she told him.

Having heard what she had to say, the superintendent told her that the body of a woman answering her sister's description had been recovered from the canal at Pendleton on February 14th. No one had so far come forward to identify the woman, and her clothes were still at Salford Workhouse.

Milne then accompanied Miss Dunn to the workhouse, where she examined the dead woman's clothes tearfully and identified them. Handed her sister's wedding ring, she began to sob.

The superintendent arranged for a policeman to take her home. Then he returned to his office and applied for

Mary Charles's body to be exhumed. Why, he wondered, hadn't her husband reported her missing? As a policeman, Luke Charles could not have failed to read and recognise her description when it was distributed to all forces in the area.

Checking the constable's background, Milne learned that in December, 1854, he had been a member of the Irish police force stationed at Maryborough Heath, near Emo, Queen's County. He had married Mary Dunn, but they had never lived together, because in Ireland policemen were not at that time allowed to marry without the consent of their commanding officers. For some reason Charles had not obtained the necessary permission, and as a result the marriage was not recognised by the police authorities. So while Charles continued to live in the police barracks Mary had remained with her brother at Celbridge, County Kildare. Charles did not visit her, but kept in touch by letter.

A few years later he had decided to join the English police, and on April 2nd, 1861, he had left Ireland and arrived at the home of his sister-in-law, Julia Dunn, at Clegg's Square, Pendleton. Having been accepted by the Lancashire Constabulary at Preston, he was assigned to the Bacup and Rossendale Division, and then on May 20th, 1862, he was sent to Bury.

In August of that year he took his two weeks' leave in Ireland and returned to England to find that his wife had arrived in Pendleton. At the end of the month the couple had gone to lodge with a widow, Sarah Porrith, in Bolton Street, Bury. There they had at last lived together as man and wife, eight years after their wedding.

Milne visited Mrs. Porrith to question her about her former lodger. She told him that the last time she and her daughter had seen Mary Charles was at about 5.30 p.m. on February 13th. Mrs. Charles had been going in the direction of Bolton Street railway station, and had said she was on her way to Pendleton to see her sister. She expected to be back at around nine o'clock that evening.

Mrs. Porrith was reasonably certain that Mrs. Charles had been wearing the brown cloak, skirt and jacket that Milne produced for her to identify.

At 9 p.m. on February 13th Luke Charles had come home alone. He'd said he was feeling ill, and instead of reporting for duty that night he went straight to bed. He hadn't said anything about where his wife was, and when Mrs. Porrith asked him about this he had mumbled something about her having gone to Ireland to visit her mother.

Milne remembered that on February 16th Charles, still pleading ill-health, had applied for leave of absence. The police surgeon had said that nothing was the matter with the constable's health, but he was granted leave anyway, and spent three days in Ireland. When he came back he left Mrs. Porrith's house for good.

Milne then learned from the stationmaster at Bolton Street station that the 5.35 p.m. train from Bury to Pendleton on February 13th had stopped at Clifton at 5.45. A passenger getting off the train at this point could easily walk to Pendleton via the canal tow-path.

The superintendent also noted that the return train from Pendleton, due in Bury at 9 p.m., had been four minutes behind schedule.

Mrs. Porrith had said that Luke Charles was home by 9 p.m., which meant that he could not have been on that train, but there were other ways he might have travelled home.

Milne went to visit Julia Dunn to find out more about her sister's married life. He learned that in August, 1862, on the day Charles was en route to Ireland, his wife, tired of waiting for him, had set out for England and the couple unknowingly passed one another at sea.

When she realised what had happened, Mary went to stay with Julia until her husband returned. On August 29th she heard that he was back in Bury, so she left her sister's house and went to join him.

However, two weeks later, on September 9th, Julia

Dunn received a letter from Mary which revealed that the reunion was not what she hoped for. Mary wrote:

"Dear Julia, I am stopping at this place you saw (Mrs. Porrith's). I sleep with the landlady, for Luke is out nine hours at night and sleeps all day. I don't see him till evening and he seems not at all pleased with my coming. He says he went to Ireland for the purpose of stopping me from coming till a further time. I am very unhappy at present. He would wish me to go home for some time longer, Mary."

Julia Dunn showed the letter to Superintendent Milne and said that she had received many more in a similar vein. The last one was dated January 31st, 1863. In it Mary complained of having a cold and her sister's lack of concern for her; *". . . and as for Charles, he pays very little heed to me. We are only on speaking terms,"* she had written.

Julia said she had not seen either her brother-in-law or Mary on February 13th. She had, however, seen her brother-in-law on February 21st when he called unexpectedly at her home. He said he was alone because Mary was too ill to travel.

Julia had been surprised by the visit as Charles had not been to her house since he'd been stationed at Bacup three years earlier. Although relations between them were not good, particularly as Julia suspected him of beating her sister, she had nevertheless made him welcome. With two friends they had gone for a drink at the Horse Shoe Inn in Pendleton, although Luke Charles had only one brandy before he said he must go.

Julia Dunn said she'd walked with him to Pendleton station where he told her, "I must make haste home. I told Mary if the doctor should call to tell him that I had only gone out for a short walk." Touched and surprised by his concern for Mary, Julia told him she was very sorry to hear that her sister was ill and that she intended to visit them both on Simnel Sunday (Mother's Day).

On March 12th, however, Charles sent her a letter telling her not to come as Mary had gone home to Ireland to visit her mother.

Julia had later discovered this was not true. Her concern turned to alarm when she heard that Luke had been giving Mary's clothes away. On May 23rd she had confronted him, demanding to be told where her sister was.

Her brother-in-law said that Mary might be with friends in County Wicklow, or if she was not there she could be with a Miss Evens in St. Mary's Street, Dublin.

"Poor girl, she must have gone away in a troubled mind not to have taken any clothes with her," Julia had remarked.

"Oh, but she did," Luke said quickly. "She took night clothing."

Julia asked him how her sister was living while she was away, and this was answered with a shrug. "If she wants support she ought to send to me."

Julia Dunn told the superintendent that even then it had not occurred to her that Mary had come to any harm. She did not go to the police until months later, following a letter her brother-in-law wrote to her:

"Dear Julia, I wonder if you have heard anything yet from Mary. I hope you have, for you appeared in a bad way about her the last time I saw you. Well, I had a letter from her yesterday saying that she is quite well and very comfortable and is stopping at present with a friend near Liverpool. I have nothing particular to speak of, so I will finish hoping this will find you quite well and in better temper than when I last saw you. Goodbye, and remaining yours truly, Luke Charles.

"P.S: I require no answer to this."

Milne returned to the police station and sent for Luke Charles, asking him where his wife was. The constable told him she had gone to stay with friends in Liverpool because Bury did not agree with her health.

Milne kept his suspicions, and his knowledge that Mary Charles was dead, to himself. He asked the constable if he coud imagine how upset his sister-in-law was. Charles said that he was sure Mary would write to her relatives if she thought this necessary.

The superintendent wanted to know what Mary Charles

was living on while she was in Liverpool, and Charles said he was sending her money by Post Office order.

Making further enquiries, Milne discovered that his constable had never sent Post Office orders to anyone. Charles, summoned again by the superintendent, said, "Oh, I did not send it through the Post Office at all. I gave the money into her hand."

Then he resigned from the police force and walked out of Milne's office.

On September 2nd Charles wrote to the superintendent:

"Sir. My reason for not telling my sister-in-law where my wife is, is in consequence of my sister-in-law being in debt. She wishes my wife to take charge of some property which she has in her possession. At least my wife told me this."

On September 7th Captain Elgee, the Chief Constable of Lancashire, called on Charles at his home. He found him lying in bed complaining of pains in his side. Elgee told him that Julia Dunn was anxious to know where Mary was and he asked for her address.

Charles said that as far as he knew, his wife was with her brother in Ireland. He didn't know his brother-in-law's address because he had moved since he'd last heard from him.

Questioned further, Charles changed his story. Mary, he said, was in Liverpool, staying with friends. He said she was well and would be angry with Julia for giving him so much trouble. Elgee suggested he should tell Mary to write at once to put Julia's mind at ease, but Charles made no response to this suggestion.

Deeply suspicious, Elgee left Charles and went straight to Superintendent Milne with his account of the interview.

Luke Charles was then arrested on suspicion of murder, and on September 14th he appeared before Bury magistrates.

Earlier that day the body was exhumed. Mary Charles's features were so well preserved that Julia Dunn identified her without hesitation.

Informed of this, the magistrates committed Charles for trial.

At Liverpool Assizes on December 21st, Mr. Monk QC, prosecuting, told the jury, "There is no direct proof of the prisoner's guilt, but the circumstantial evidence against him is strong."

Charles pleaded not guilty, but Superintendent Milne had been busy tracking down witnesses.

The first to be called by the prosecution was a young Irishwoman, beautiful Ellen Ford. She said she had known Luke Charles for six years in Ireland. When she'd first met him he was in the police, stationed at Maryborough Heath, about three miles from her home.

After a two-year courtship he had asked her to marry him. Unaware that she already had a wife, she had accepted his proposal.

He was later transferred to Ballybrittis but still managed to visit her regularly. A year later he decided to leave Ireland to join the police in England. He wanted to earn more money so they could be married, but the court was told that at the same time he was also writing to Mary, telling her he was moving to England so that they could be together.

In August 1862 Charles returned to Ireland with the news that he had saved enough money to marry Ellen. But because he had no certificate from his parish priest in Bury declaring him to be single, Father O'Connel wouldn't marry them.

Charles went back to England, promising to return. Six months later, in the middle of February, 1863, he came briefly to Ireland to assure Ellen they would soon be married. A further six months passed before his next visit on August 1st.

Ellen was disappointed that he had still not managed to get the certificate, but they nevertheless went to see Father Hooney in the hope that he would marry them anyway. The priest was prepared to do so without a certificate, and said a letter would suffice. He then wrote to his opposite number in Bury, Father John Fraser, asking him if Charles were single, but Fraser replied saying he didn't know. Hooney therefore told the couple he could not marry them.

It was a bitter blow but Luke Charles was determined not to leave Ellen behind a fourth time. On August 7th they travelled to Bury together, believing they would find a more obliging priest.

At first Ellen lodged with Charles at Mrs. Elizabeth Whittington's house. They slept in separate rooms, she emphasised. Charles stayed with her there for two days, and then moving out to lodge at Mrs. Balfe's, where Ellen visited him every day, having her meals with him. After a week she also moved to Mrs. Balfe's. The pair thought it wrong to live in such physical proximity while they were unwed, so they agreed that Ellen should stay with her married sister in Coniston, in the Lake District, until Charles had 'regulated his affairs.'

It emerged that local gossip and some letters found at Charles's lodgings had led the police to Ellen Ford.

The prosecution claimed that because of his wish to marry Ellen, Luke Charles had murdered his wife.

Michael Dunn, a labourer from Celbridge, County Kildare, told the court that Charles had married his sister Mary at Christmas, 1854. Charles hadn't applied for permission from the police authorities, as he and Mary had not been allowed to make a home together at the police barracks.

The witness said that Mary had lived with him for the next eight years, during which her husband had not visited her even once.

Then on August 8th, 1862, after a long silence, Luke Charles sent Mary a letter in which he said he was living in Bury, and that if he succeeded in getting leave, she would see him towards the end of the month. Otherwise he would write again to her on September 1st, to let her know what she was to do about joining him in England.

However, in a later letter he referred to "your

comfortable home," asking, "had you not better stay in it?"

That same August, Mary, tired of waiting for her husband to send for her, had gone alone to England. Michael said he had not seen her since.

Until the end of August, 1862, Charles had lodged with Mrs. Maria Nuttall, who now told the court that she remembered him going to Ireland in that month in order to bring his wife over. However, shortly after he left, Mrs. Charles had arrived on the doorstep looking for him.

Mrs. Nuttall didn't take married couples, so when Charles got back from Ireland they moved to Mrs. Porrith's in Bolton Street.

Mrs. Nuttall said she kept up a friendship with Mary because she felt sorry for her. One afternoon they met in the street and Mary confided that she had found letters in her husband's box signed "Ellen." This bothered her so much that she was now sorry she had ever come to England.

She had gone on to say that she was scared that Luke would do something to her if she did not leave him.

Father John Fraser of St. Joseph's Roman Catholic Church in Bury, told the court that Charles had asked him for a certificate declaring he was a single man in the summer of 1863. Father Fraser had declined because he didn't know him well enough to be in a position to say whether he was single or not.

Making discreet enquiries, he learned that Charles was in fact married. But as the priest was told this in confidence he was unable to disclose it. So when Father Hooney wrote from Ireland asking if Charles were married, Father Fraser replied that he did not know.

The court then heard that when Mary's corpse was re-examined it was found to display marks which could not have been made after death. Bruises and scratches on the wrists and neck must have been made either before or immediately after Mary entered the water, and certainly before her circulation had stopped.

There was also evidence, the prosecution claimed, of a struggle. For when Mrs. Charles was pulled from the canal her hair was dishevelled, the sleeve of her jacket was torn at the shoulder and part of the trimming had been pulled off.

The defence, however, said that all these signs of a "struggle" could have been caused by the grappling-iron used to retrieve the body.

Mr. Holker, defending, claimed that Ellen Ford was a scheming woman who would stop at nothing to get her man. Luke Charles had come to England in order to get out of her clutches, but she was so determined to have him that she had come to England with Charles even after Father Hooney had refused to marry them.

If Charles had known that Mary was dead, wouldn't he simply have claimed her body, shed hypocritical tears over her grave, and then married Ellen Ford? Why go on saying that she was still alive unless he really believed it?

The defence counsel then suggested that Mary Charles, distressed by her husband's infidelity, had committed suicide. Or she could have been robbed and murdered on her way to her sister's house at Pendleton.

Summing-up, Mr. Justice Willes said that if Mary Charles had been wearing her crinoline — found on the tow-path — it would have buoyed her up. The jury had to decide whether her clothes were removed by someone contemplating suicide or someone contemplating murder.

Twenty minutes later the jury returned to find Luke Charles guilty of his wife's murder. Sentenced to death, he was taken to Liverpool's Kirkdale Prison where he was reported to seem not the least depressed by the thought of what awaited him.

"He eats and sleeps well, and converses freely with all who approach him," said a warder.

He still maintained he was innocent, but a petition launched for a reprieve was signed mostly by barristers who felt that there was no concrete evidence against him.

There was no reprieve, and on Saturday, January 9th, 1864, fewer than 200 people turned up to watch Luke

Charles's execution. Spectators were expected to arrive from Bury, but the railway company had failed to advertise their special excursion train, so it ran all but empty.

At a minute before noon, Luke Charles mounted the scaffold. Seconds later William Calcraft despatched him. Charles fell with a crash which sent dust flying from the scaffold and tried the strength of the woodwork.

"Poor fellow!" murmured some of the crowd.

"What the heck are you talking about?" another spectator shouted. "He's only a bobby!"

25

WHY DID HE CUT THE SCHOOLTEACHER'S THROAT?

"What's think about yon tockus?"

MOTIVELESS MURDERS seem to be accepted as a modern concept, stemming from the high-rise flats, overcrowding, unemployment and the alienation many people feel in our "high tech" society. But Victorian England had its fair share of motiveless murders, such as this case, which occurred in the pretty rural village of Belmont, near Bolton in Lancashire.

On the morning of Saturday, November 15th, 1890, young Clement Talbot was out playing with his dog in a lonely wooded spot called Longworth Clough when he came upon the mangled corpse of his schoolteacher, Elizabeth Ann Holt. In death she was ghastly to behold. Her head had been kicked in, her throat slashed, and the clothes had been torn from her body as if, to quote one contemporary newspaper report on the crime, "she had been the victim of a ferocious attack by some wild animal."

The body was taken to her mother's cottage in the village of Egerton, where Dr. Robinson performed an immediate post-mortem examination. In his opinion she had been dead for about a week and her death was due to appalling head and throat wounds. But although her clothes, particularly her underwear, had been ripped to pieces, there had been no attempt at rape.

Miss Holt, 21, had lived with her mother and younger

sister, Sarah, in Egerton. She worked as a teacher at Belmont village school, a few miles from her home.

Because of the distance involved in travelling every day, it had been her habit to stay in Belmont at the house of the schoolmaster, Henry Swayles, and his family from Monday until Friday. On Friday evening she always went back home to Egerton for the weekend. She used invariably to walk back to Belmont on Monday mornings, along a road that took her close to Longworth Clough.

Sarah Holt tearfully told the police that on Monday, November 10th, her sister Lizzie had left home as usual at 7.30. She had with her some parcels of food and clothing. Neither she nor her mother had known until the following Saturday, when she was found dead, that Lizzie had not been at school all week. As Miss Holt had been neither raped nor robbed (her parcels and purse were found intact by her body), the police were at a loss as to a motive for her murder. They asked Sarah if Lizzie had had any enemies, but the girl replied firmly that she had been very popular and well liked by everyone.

Henry Swayles, schoolmaster at the National School in Belmont, told the police that although Miss Holt had not arrived at the school on November 10th, he hadn't thought there was anything worrying in her staying away. She had done so twice before, he explained, and sent him notice each time. However, although he had not heard from her at all during that week he had still not thought it necessary to contact her home.

A farmer, Robert Scholes, told the police that on the morning of November 10th he had been driving his milk cart along Longworth Lane when he saw Lizzie Holt, whom he knew well, walking towards Belmont. A moment later, he said, he spotted a local ruffian by the name of Thomas Macdonald walking about 150 yards behind the pretty teacher, and going in the same direction. Another farmer, Rowland Heaton, also remembered having seen the pair walking along Longworth Lane, some distance apart, but going towards Belmont. It had been raining, he recalled, and Miss Holt had had her umbrella up.

Thomas Macdonald, 32, was well known to the local police as a violent criminal. At 20 he had waylaid a girl on the moors and raped her; a crime for which he was sentenced to 10 years penal servitude. After serving only eight he was released for good behaviour and had gone to live in Egerton, supported mainly by his long-suffering aunt, Mrs. Honor Bann. Except for some casual work at Longworth Collieries, he spent most of his time idling around the village, drinking and getting into fights. It was a pastime for which he periodically ended up in the cells.

The police already had reason to suspect Macdonald of having blood on his hands, because a few weeks before Miss Holt's murder he had been drinking in Bolton with a young navvy named Mather. The following day Mather was found dead, floating in Belmont reservoir.

Macdonald was arrested for his involvement on a charge of manslaughter, but owing to lack of evidence he'd had to be released.

Thus police were not surprised to find that Macdonald was again the suspect in the Holt murder. That same evening P.C. Hargreaves and Sergeant Hayward went to his aunt's house to arrest him. "Tom," said Hayward when Thomas Macdonald opened the door. "You are going to be taken into custody on suspicion of having caused the death of Elizabeth Ann Holt at Longworth Clough."

"I was there," replied Macdonald, "but I did her no harm. You will have to find another for this." He was then taken away to Bolton police station.

Once there Macdonald was closely interrogated about his movements on November 10th. He admitted he had been to Belmont in the morning, and that he had seen Miss Holt, whom he knew by sight, walking along Longworth Lane in front of him. But he claimed he had overtaken her and gone on to Belmont, where he had worked that day at the Longworth Collieries until evening, and after being paid he had got drunk, for which he had been arrested. He had spent the night in the cells of the local police station.

John Brierley, the underground manager at Longworth Collieries, told the police that he knew Macdonald well, but said he had certainly not employed him on November 10th.

P.C. Golightly, however, verified that he had arrested Macdonald on the evening of November 10th for being drunk and disorderly. He remembered that Macdonald had been in quite a state, with blood on his clothes, a scar over his left cheek and a bleeding lip. When questioned about his wounds, Macdonald had plausibly explained that he had been in a fight earlier that day.

Meanwhile, as the police investigations continued, Macdonald's clothes were sent to Frank Paul, the professor of medical jurisprudence at the University College, Liverpool, for examination. He found blood marks on the man's clogs, penknife and the sleeves and cuff of his jacket.

If the police needed any more proof in order to charge Macdonald it came when his Aunt Honor told police that he had confessed to her that he had murdered Miss Holt. On November 19th, therefore, Macdonald was formally charged with her murder, and replied, "I will say nothing here."

Macdonald's trial took place at Liverpool Assizes on December 13th, 1890, before Mr. Justice Cave. Mr. Cottingham was elected to defend him.

The newspapers reported that there was a great deal of interest in the case, adding intriguingly that, "in marked contrast to previous murder trials in the same building, not a single woman was permitted to enter the court."

The prosecution had a very strong case against Macdonald, and as witness after witness took the stand it grew stronger.

Dr. Robinson, who had performed the post-mortem at her home, told the court that besides having severe head wounds Miss Holt's throat had been cut by a small, sharp cutting instrument similar to a penknife belonging to Macdonald.

Jane Marsden, a neighbour of Macdonald's, told the court that at about 9.30 on the morning of November 10th, she had seen Macdonald come up the road from the direction of Belmont and go into his aunt's house. As he passed by her window, she said, she had noticed how dirty and sullied-looking he was, as if he had been working all night.

Thomas Maclean, overlooker at Ashton Mill where Mrs. Bann, Macdonald's aunt, was employed, recalled how Macdonald had come to the mill on the morning of November 10th looking rather excited. He had had his right hand up to his face, but there was no sign of any blood. "What does thee want here, Tom?" Maclean had asked, "surely, thee's not looking for work?" Macdonald hadn't been amused. "Go and tell my auntie she's wanted up yonder straight away," he'd said sharply. After Maclean had brought Mrs. Bann, she put on her shawl and hurried away with her nephew. Maclean assumed they were going home.

Honor Bann was next to give evidence. She told the court that when she'd left for work on the morning of the murder her nephew was still in the house. Later in the day she had been very surprised when Maclean came up and said he was outside, asking for her. At first Macdonald explained his visit by telling her that she was needed at home immediately. He told her some story that someone had arrived at the house from America to see her. However, when they had got some distance from the mill, he had suddenly confessed to her that he had committed a murder.

Stunned, Mrs. Bann had asked him who he'd murdered, for it never occurred to her to doubt him. So he told her it was Lizzie Holt.

Mr. Cottingham, defending, butted in at this point. "Did your nephew actually say he had murdered Lizzie Holt?" Mrs. Bann thought for a moment, then nodded. "I have told the truth and cannot get over it."

"What was your reaction to the confession?" asked Cottingham, and Mrs. Bann, wiping tears from her cheeks, said, " I told him to go drown his self afore he brought more disgrace on the family."

To this Macdonald had replied that he was going to give himself up. Then he'd turned from her and walked away.

She had gone back to work and told no one about what he had said. At 5 o'clock she said she went home but her nephew wasn't there. He didn't return until the following day, when he told her he had spent the night at the police station after being arrested for drunkenness.

She'd heard nothing more about the murder until he was arrested at her house on the following Saturday evening. During that week, however, she had asked him if she could wash his shirt, and he told her he had already done it himself.

"Was this usual?" asked the prosecutor. "Had he on other occasions washed his shirt?" "No, never," admitted Mrs. Bann.

During their investigation the police had tried very hard to discover if there had been any quarrel between Lizzie Holt and Macdonald, but though the two had lived in the same village it seemed they had never even spoken to one another.

However, they did find some witnesses who were willing to testify to the hostile feelings Macdonald harboured for the dead girl.

John Henry, a friend of Macdonald's, told the court that Tom had once boasted to him that many people in Egerton were scared of him, and that Lizzie Holt in particular feared him to the extent that whenever she saw him coming she always rushed away. He had told this story with some glee, the witness said.

Richard Radcliffe told the court that once, on November 3rd, while he and Macdonald were talking together in Longworth Lane, Miss Holt had suddenly passed them by on her way to Belmont. Macdonald, looking up, had said, lewdly, referring very pointedly to the girl, "What's think about yon tockus [backside]? I should like to take the pride out o' yon." John Lee had also overheard this conversation, but he thought it had been made jokingly and did not think much more about it.

There was a sensation in the court when two confessions Macdonald had made to the officers at Bolton Road police station on November 25th and 26th were read out in court:

"At eight o'clock on the morning of November tenth, I started from home to go over to Belmont to see the manager at Longworth Collieries about work. On Longworth Lane I overtook the deceased. As soon as I overtook her, I got hold of her shoulder. I asked her what she had been telling lies about me for. I told her that she had set it out that I'd followed her a few weeks ago for the purpose of doing her harm. She told me to let go of her shoulder. I told her I would not do so until she had retracted what she had said. She jerked her shoulder away out of my hand, shut her umbrella, took hold of the small end of it and struck me with it. I became enraged, threw her down and beat her about the head and cut her throat.

"Then I dragged her across the land and down into Longworth Clough. I cut open her clothes to see if her heart was still beating. I found it did not beat. I then went home."

He denied that he had tried to rape her. "A great many people think this girl was simply got hold of for the purpose of ravishing her, but I can swear on my dying oath such is not the case."

The day after making that statement, November 26th, Macdonald had made another, in which he added more details:

"Man, I had a job with her. When she struck me with the umbrella on the head, she might have got away, for I was quiet for a few minutes. The first time I knocked her down she got up and I had to put my leg behind hers before I got her down the second time. I soon finished her off then with my clogs and the knife. When I took her to the bottom of the clough I was nearly making a mess of myself. When I was halfway home I was looking for my knife to cut some tobacco. I had to go back for it, and when I went back for it I found it underneath the body."

The reading out of these two statements caused an understandable uproar in the courtroom.

Mr. Cottingham now pleaded for Macdonald's life.

"There is no doubt he is guilty of a cruel and violent homicide," he said. "But I plead not for an acquittal, not for the establishment of innocence, I plead for life alone."

Pale and haggard, Macdonald, who had harangued witnesses and counsel alike throughout the proceedings, suddenly got to his feet and shouted out, "I don't want it. I am guilty straight off. Let it drop."

The jury retired and half an hour later found Macdonald guilty of wilful murder. He heard the verdict and subsequent sentence of death without uncharacteristically for him betraying any emotion.

The prisoner was removed to Kirkdale Prison, where he was visited by his long-suffering aunt, Mrs. Honor Bann. She found him very depressed and refusing to talk about the murder except to say that he was glad he had not taken Miss Holt's purse. Mrs. Bann's visit was made all the more frustrating by the presence of a thick iron grating, which traditionally separated relatives from condemned men, making it impossible for them to embrace or kiss, so Macdonald stood all the time, pressing himself as close to the bars as possible. When it was time for her to leave Macdonald suddenly collapsed. Mrs. Bann, seeing her nephew in such a distressed state, also became upset and was led away in tears.

Thomas Macdonald's execution was set for the last day of the year, Wednesday, December 31st, 1890. Minutes before the hanging, Berry, the executioner, suddenly realised he had forgotten to bring the white cap which is traditionally put over the condemned man's head immediately prior to his execution. In something of a dilemma, he asked two reporters, there to witness the execution, if he could borrow their handkerchiefs. The reporters, somewhat taken aback by this macabre request, obliged, and Berry tied the handkerchiefs together. He tried it out on one of the reporters, but it was too tight. "Well," sighed Berry. "I shall have to do without. I have hanged them without a cap before and I must do it again."

However, when the time came for the hanging the reporters noticed that Berry had manufactured a white cap apparently made from an old towel. As he slipped it over Macdonald's head the condemned man was heard to murmur, "Lord Jesus, receive my soul." The lever was then drawn. The execution was over in exactly a minute. When the doctor got down into the pit beneath the gallows to feel for Macdonald's pulse, he noted that it took just one minute for him to stop breathing.

Macdonald was buried under the footpath close to the coach-house where his execution had taken place.

How did a minor disagreement between two people who hardly knew each other come to end in brutal, sadistic murder?

Perhaps the clue to this can be found in the personalities of killer and victim. Thomas Macdonald was a violent man with very little self-control, and like many such people, had a deep resentment of authority. In her position as a schoolteacher, Miss Holt would certainly have represented authority to him, and was also, in his opinion haughty and proud. This enraged him to such a pitch that he wanted to "take the pride out o' yon." When he grabbed her shoulder in Longworth Lane it was probably to do just that, but verbally. It is unlikely he had really intended to murder her. However, when she resisted and hit him over the head with her umbrella, probably telling him exactly what she thought of him, he must have completely lost control of himself and murder was the only possible outcome.